Self Presentatio

C

C

Titles in the *Macmillan Modern Office* Series

Business Administration III Pack	McFetridge
Count on Confidence: The Way in to Personal Effectiveness	Chisholm
Elementary Exercises in Word Processing – Student's Book, Teacher's Book	Brown & Tiffney
English Language Skills	Hughes
Integrated Assignments in Secretarial, Office and Business Procedures Pack	McFetridge
Intermediate Exercises in Word Processing – Student's Book, Teacher's Book	Brown & Tiffney
Quickly into QWERTY	Hughes
Self Presentation Skills	Hughes & Weller
Starting in the Office Pack	Barnes

Easily into . . .

dBase III Plus (Exercise disks available)	Gosling
Desk Top Publishing	Gosling
DisplayWrite 4	Gosling
DOS (Exercise disks available)	Gosling
LocoScript for the Amstrad PCW	Rogers
Lotus 1–2–3	Gilligan
MultiMate Advantage II	Gosling
MultiMate Advantage II Advanced	Gosling
WordStar	Simons
WordStar 1512	Gosling
WordStar 2000 Release 2	Simons
WordStar 2000 Advanced	Simons
WordStar 2000 Release 3	Simons

Macmillan Modern Office

Series Editor: Christine Simons

SELF PRESENTATION SKILLS

Vera Hughes and David Weller

MACMILLAN

First published 1991 by
THE MACMILLAN PRESS LTD
Houndmills, Basingstoke, Hampshire RG21 2XS
and London
Companies and representatives
throughout the world

ISBN 0–333–53772–6

A catalogue record for this book is available
from the British Library.

Printed in Hong Kong

10   9   8   7   6   5   4   3   2
00 99 98 97 96 95 94 93 92

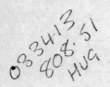

Contents

Acknowledgements

The chapter on 'Oral Assessment' could not have been written without the willing help and expertise of Jim Sweetman, Chief Examiner for the Midland Examining Group, GCSE English syllabus. The authors would like to thank him and to recommend his various publications in that area of work.

Introduction

Is this book for you?

Did you know that up to 60% of the messages you convey when you are talking with someone face-to-face is through your body language? Did you know that the way in which you present yourself in all sorts of situations has a great effect on the outcome? Did you know that this applies in all aspects of your working life, from your first oral assessment or job interview to representing your organisation or company in a media interview?

If you want to improve your Self Presentation Skills in a wide variety of situations, this book *is* for you.

What will you learn from this book?

The book will help you think about what preparations you should make, how best to get your message across and how to avoid some of the pitfalls in self presentation.

You will learn how to approach people, how to talk to people and how to put forward your point of view. You will be encouraged to study your own body language and to analyse the image you project.

The book does not give hard and fast rules about how to behave in given situations, because no two situations are alike. Rather, it gives hints and tips on what to look out for and how to show yourself at your best.

How does it work?

It works in two ways. You can work through it from beginning to end to get an overall picture of how to present yourself.

You can use it to prepare yourself for specific situations, and to check afterwards on how well or badly you thought you did.

Like its companion *English Language Skills* by Vera Hughes, you can use it in the most suitable way for you.

At the beginning of each chapter you will find a list of the main points covered – these are a repeat of the points written in the Contents table. Some chapters lend themselves to definite 'Practice' exercises; others do not because you can only really learn by doing whatever it is for real. Where practice exercises are relevant, they are included. At the end of each chapter there is a list of 'Points to remember'; these are useful for checking that you have made all the preparations you should and for self-analysis after the event.

Situations covered in the book

A very wide range of situations is covered. The first two chapters, about body language and getting a conversation off to a good start, are important in every situation – even on the telephone. Read these as a basis for the rest of the book.

After that the situations start in your school or college days with a chapter on oral assessment, and progress through everyday activities, such as talking to customers or clients, to first level management situations, such as showing someone how to do something or attending meetings.

The last three chapters are about situations where you are definitely in control as a manager or leader or are representing your whole organisation.

There has to be a first time for you in every situation.

What this book is not

This is not a book which will teach you about power dressing, colour, line and style of clothes or makeup. Of course the importance of appearance is emphasised, but there are several publications or counselling services which will help you make the best of yourself in that sense.

This book will help you make the best of yourself physically and verbally.

1 Body Language

In this chapter:
- Body language is important
- Posture – standing, sitting, positioning yourself
- Legs and feet
- Arms
- Hands
- Face and eyes
- Interpreting the signals
- Personal space
- Image

Body language is important

This book is about presenting yourself well in all sorts of situations. It is about communication, inter-personal skills and image.

When we communicate, up to 60% of the messages we send is through our body language – what we do with our arms, hands, legs, eyes, faces and general posture. The other 40% is made up of the tone of voice we use (about 30%) and the words we use (10%). This is why this is the first chapter in the book: the messages we send to other people through our body language are so important, except of course on the telephone. Even then, the way we sit, stand and look affects the tone of voice, as you will see in Chapter 5 – On the Telephone.

As you work through this book, or as you concentrate on particular parts of it, you will be reminded of how important your body language is, and how, if you control it, you can present yourself much more effectively. Control of your own body language will help you succeed in oral assessments, talk to and listen to people well, contribute to a meeting or address a group – in fact it will help you in every situation mentioned in this book and in other situations too.

One of the fascinating, and alarming, things about body language is that it takes over. Once your brain is in gear and you are talking to someone or listening to them, all your body language messages are subconscious, and you might be sending out all sorts of messages you do not want to convey. This is why it is so important to learn and practise a few basic rules about how and where you stand, sit, look etc, so that at least you start off a conversation in control of your body and the messages it is sending.

Posture

You have probably heard people say you should 'stand tall', 'stand up straight' and 'not slouch'. This is because, whether you are standing or sitting, you should look confident, interested and alert. If you look confident, people will have confidence in you.

Standing

Look at this drawing. You cannot see the expression on the faces of these two people, but you can tell immediately that one is in control of the situation and the other is not.

The person on the left is standing with head up (but not tilted backwards or sideways) shoulders square, hands at sides and legs firmly planted, feet slightly apart. The person on the right is standing with head slightly bent, drooping shoulders and one leg slightly bent, giving an overall impression of being unsure and not at all confident. If you wanted to ask one of these people the way, which do you think would be the more likely to know?

Give yourself, and other people, a feeling of confidence by standing straight and standing tall.

Sitting

The same applies to the way you sit. You should sit looking interested and confident and relaxed, but not too laid-back. Look at these three drawings and see the difference.

The person on the left is sitting looking very laid-back; look where his bottom is – halfway along the chair. This means that his body has literally got to be 'laid-back' for his back to reach the back of the chair. His legs, arms and hands are conveying the same

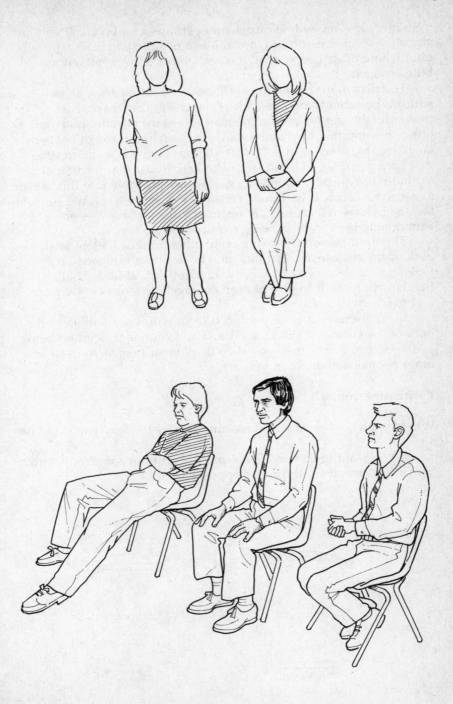

message, too – relaxed, laid-back and perhaps a bit bored. If you are already a confident sort of person, it is a posture you can easily slip into, telling other people that you are, perhaps, over-relaxed and a little arrogant.

The person in the middle is sitting in a relaxed way, as well, with his bottom against the back of the chair. This makes him sit more upright and he looks more alert. He is even leaning forward a little, showing that he is interested. He is saying, through his body language, to someone else, "What you are saying is so interesting that I am prepared to lean forward to hear it just that fraction of a second more quickly." Someone else would probably rate this person as a good listener. If he leaned forward any more, he would probably look aggressive. His hands are resting calmly and his legs are comfortably bent without being too open or too closed.

The third person is looking quite different. His bottom is at the back of the chair again, but this time he is sitting hunched up looking very tense. His legs are close together and he is holding hands with himself to give himself courage. He looks very unsure and nervous.

In some chairs it is very difficult to sit with your bottom at the back of the chair and still look relaxed and confident, without being laid-back, but that is how you should try to sit to give yourself and other people confidence in you.

Positioning yourself

Where you stand or sit is just as important as the way you stand or sit.

If you want to be very direct or even confront somebody with something, stand or sit directly opposite them.

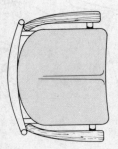 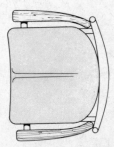

You will be in an eyeball to eyeball situation, particularly if you are close together.

Sometimes you need to stand or sit alongside somebody to show them something, but you will find it very difficult to maintain eye contact in that position.

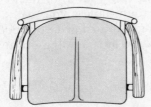 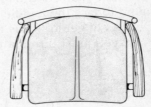

It is often better to sit or stand at a slight angle to someone, so you can both hear and see what the other is trying to say. At the same time neither feels threatened or distant.

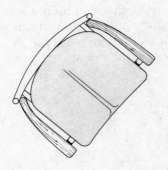 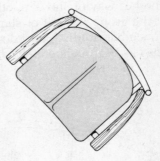

Of course, if you turn away from other people, you are cutting them out, showing that you are not interested in what they are saying or doing. As soon as you turn your back effective communication becomes very difficult. You can see from this drawing that the person on the end of the group just does not want to know.

If you find yourself in that position, turn round, or turn your chair round to face the middle of the group, unless you really want to tell the others to get lost. It is not enough to turn just your body or your chair, you must turn both, and if you are standing up, turn your feet as well.

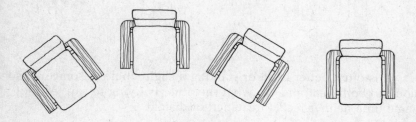

Another way of showing other people that you do not want to be part of the group is to sit or stand slightly outside it. You can see which member of this group does not want to be part of it, or perhaps has been deliberately shut out by the others.

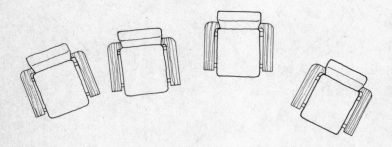

If you find yourself in this position, move your chair or yourself into the group, if you want to be part of it.

Part of the secret of controlling your body language is to be aware of it and how and where you are standing or sitting. If you are aware of what you are doing, and something is wrong, you can do something to put it right. This applies to posture, positioning and all the different parts of your body as well.

Legs and feet

As you saw with the drawings of the people on page 3, what you do with your legs and feet is also sending messages to other people.

Some people say that if you sit with your legs crossed, you are sending 'closed' messages to other people, and so you are to some extent. It depends firstly on whether you are a man or a woman, and secondly on the general position you find yourself in. For example, if you are sitting on an upright chair, and your feet can hardly touch the ground, it is often more comfortable to sit with your legs crossed. If you are sitting in a very low, easy chair, crossing your legs can make you look very inelegant or too laid-back or both.

For obvious reasons women tend to cross their legs more than men do, particularly if they are sitting with a space in front of them.

If you feel comfortable sitting with your legs crossed, then sit like that. Do not hoist your ankles round each other, which makes you look very self-protective and negative – as if you are keeping everything crossed!

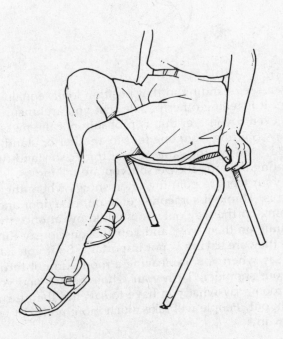

As you can see, standing in that position looks equally negative and defensive. It is telling other people that you are unsure of yourself, and even if you are, that is probably not the message you want to convey. Shifting from one foot to another or standing on one leg, like a child, conveys the same sort of thing, so stand firm, with your feet pointing towards the person you are talking to.

The way your feet are pointing often shows where the focus of your attention is. Think of someone going out of a door and turning to say something on the way out. You will know at once that they are going to continue on their way, and you subconsciously think that perhaps what they are saying is not important. So if you have something to say when you are leaving a room, do not throw the remark over your shoulder. Turn your whole body – and your feet – back into the room, say what you have to say and then turn back again and walk out. People will take much more notice of what you say. Try it, it works.

Arms

What should you do with your arms when you are standing talking to someone? If you stand with your arms folded, you will look very closed and negative, and the higher up your body your arms go, the more negative you appear to be. Yet it is very comfortable to stand or sit with your arms folded, and very difficult to stand with them by your side, because you feel very open and vulnerable. From the drawing below it is quite clear which of these two people is the more confident, open and welcoming.

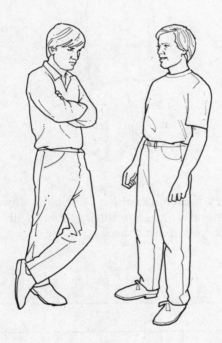

Folding your arms is putting up a little barrier between you and the outside world. If you have something to carry in your arms, you have a half-barrier, so you probably feel more comfortable.

Try to stand with your arms at your sides or to sit with your hands and arms relaxed, not folded. It is difficult, so practise it consciously.

What does this drawing convey?

Standing with your hands behind your back shows not only confidence, but authority. You are totally 'open' with nothing to hide and look as though you are in charge.

Hands

What you do with your hands can be very revealing to someone who learns how to read the messages.

Rubbing your eye can mean that you do not want to see what is going on. Rubbing your ear can mean that you do not want to hear what is being said. Putting your hand in front of your mouth can mean that you are not sure of what you are saying and want to hide it – perhaps what you are saying is not quite the truth.

So it is better to keep your hands away from your face when you are talking to someone. Particularly try not to cover your mouth,

because it will make it harder for the other person to hear what you are saying.

You should not fidget with your hands, or with other items. For one thing it is irritating to other people, and again it shows that you are unsure of yourself. If you clasp your hands tightly, it is like going on a white-knuckle ride – you are holding your own hand to give yourself courage. If you clench your fists you are showing that you are becoming quite angry, or even aggressive.

What should you do with your hands? Try to keep them relaxed, with open palms upwards. Open palms is the sign of peace. This will show other people that you are open to their ideas. If you clench your fists and fold your arms, they will immediately know that you do not agree. If you see someone doing that, you will need to change tack, and put forward your point of view in a different way.

You can use your hands in a very positive way, by shaking hands with other people when it is right to do so – when you are meeting them for the first time or leaving them, for example. It is amazing how a firm and confident handshake will begin to break

down barriers between you and other people. Avoid the
bone-crusher or the wet fish variety, if you can, and try not to be too
dominant by offering your hand palm down, or too submissive by
offering your hand palm up. Look at these drawings, and begin to
notice how other people shake hands with each other, and with you.

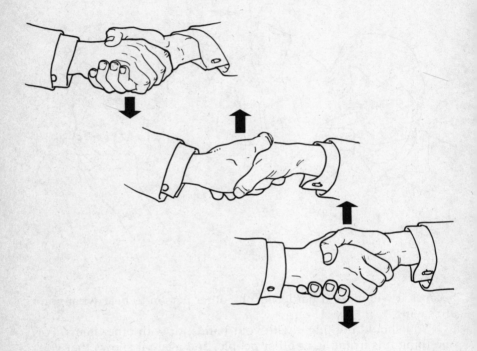

Face and eyes

The expression on your face, and particularly in your eyes, is
probably the strongest body language signal of all.

The few lines of these drawings convey so much. Think how
much more the human face conveys.

If you want to be thought of as a friendly, open sort of person,
it is important to smile. There are a lot of overworked sayings about
smiling, like 'smile and the world smiles with you' or 'a smile isn't

worth anything until you give it away', and sometimes you get really fed up with someone who is always smiling and cheerful. Yet it is important to smile, in all sorts of situations.

When you are smiling, smile with your eyes as well. Do not let the smile freeze halfway up your face, because your eyes will convey what you are *really* feeling, and a smile with only the mouth looks insincere.

As a child, you will almost certainly have heard people say, "Look at me when I'm talking to you!" Eye contact is important – very important. It shows people that you are really paying attention, that you are confident enough to look them straight in the eye and that you are not afraid to let them see what you are thinking and feeling.

Try to look people straight in the eye, not down your nose, which looks arrogant (see bottom figure on page 14).

There are occasions when you should consciously break off eye contact to let people have a rest from your gaze (this is partly why we blink). If someone is in distress, for example, look away for a moment while they compose themselves. If someone breaks off eye contact with you, and is trying to sort something out (see top figure on page 14), that is the time to stop talking and let the other person have a think. If you go jabbering on, the person will not hear and understand what you are saying anyway.

Breaking all eye contact to have a think

Looking down your nose, like a camel

Interpreting the signals

Other people's

As we said at the beginning of this chapter, body language takes over once you are concentrating on what you are saying, so it is important to practise controlling your body language. You can also have some fun – and improve your communication skills – by doing some people watching, and interpreting the messages other people are sending each other, and to you. If you are doing this, there is one important thing to remember:

Look for a cluster of signals

If you rely on one signal to tell you what someone else is thinking or feeling, you might get it wrong. For example, if they are standing with their arms folded, they might be cold rather than negative. If they are rubbing their eye, they might be having problems with a contact lens. So look for a cluster of signals if you are consciously watching other people's body language. You will be picking up the signals sub-consciously anyway.

Your own

As far as your own body language is concerned, try to be aware of it and control it. If you feel enthusiastic, then look enthusiastic with your face, your eyes and your whole body. If you feel concerned, do not be afraid to look concerned.

At the same time, try not to convey messages you would rather other people did not read. If you feel nervous, try to stand or sit in a confident manner, and you will find that you actually feel more confident. If you feel angry, try to look calm with your face and your body, and you will find yourself calming down anyway.

Try to make your body language match what you are really feeling, if the feelings are positive. If you are feeling negative, try to make your body act in a positive way.

Personal space

We all have round us a little area of personal space, and we feel threatened if someone enters our personal space uninvited. Some people feel uncomfortable if other people touch them and meeting a stranger's eye can be embarrassing. These are two ways of invading someone's personal space – by touch and by eye contact. This is why we try to avoid touching each other in a crowd or as we pass on the pavement.

At work it is important to be aware of other people's personal space, and not to enter that space uninvited. Here are a few DOs and DON'Ts which will make you and other people feel more comfortable.

DO
- approach someone from the front, if possible, not from the side or from behind. Take the trouble to walk round to the front so that they can see you coming

- let someone take something from you rather than thrusting it at them. If you offer it and

DON'T
- stand too close to people

- hover behind someone just out of their view

- touch people if either of you feels uncomfortable about it

- stare at people while they are working

they accept it, they will draw it in to their own personal space

- touch someone to show sympathy or understanding, provided you both feel comfortable about it

- shake hands, if appropriate. It is a good way of breaking down barriers and entering someone's personal space without giving offence

- jostle people as you move about. Stand aside to let them pass, if necessary

- lean over someone's shoulder, if you can help it

No-one likes anyone who is thoughtless or forceful in a physical way. Have respect for other people's personal space.

Image

All through this book we shall be suggesting that you think about the image you present to other people in different situations. Presenting the right image for the time and place is all part of the skill of self presentation.

When we talk about image, we mean the whole of you and your immediate personal belongings. We shall be thinking about hair, clothes, shoes, makeup (where appropriate!), bags, transport and so on. We are not suggesting that you should try to be what you are not, but that your total image should be recognisable for what it is. For example, a smart outfit is spoiled by dirty or worn-down shoes; a suit can sometimes be quite out-of-place.

Your image is all part of the total you that you are presenting – voice, body language, everything.

Practice

1 Look at your own body language now. How are you sitting (or standing)? What are you doing with your legs, feet, arms, hands, face and eyes? Be aware of the messages you are conveying.

2 Think of a situation in which you know you are likely to be nervous or unsure of yourself. If you are about to be in one of those situations do this for real, otherwise think about what you should do.

Decide how and where you are going to sit or stand. What are you going to do with your legs, feet, arms and hands? Where should you be looking? What sort of expression should you have on your face? If you go into a situation well-prepared, you are much more likely to succeed.

3 Do some conscious people watching. Sit quietly where there are lots of people – in a train, a pub, an airport, at a sporting event, for example – and try to identify:
- what relationship people are to each other
- if they are in a group, who is the group leader and which, if any, is slightly outside the group.

4 Watch people on television. Look at what the professionals do, particularly with their arms and hands: compare them with

people being interviewed or in game shows who are not trained to appear in front of the camera. If you are watching a play, a film or a sitcom, turn the sound off and see if you can understand what is happening by seeing what the professional actors do with their eyes, arms, hands, feet and so on.

Points to remember from this chapter

- Sit or stand straight and look confident
- Stand or sit in the right place
- Sitting with crossed legs is OK, except if it looks inelegant or uptight
- Your feet often show where your attention is
- Decide what to do with your arms and hands – and practise doing it
- Keep your hands away from your face
- Smile, if appropriate
- Maintain eye contact in most circumstances
- Look for a cluster of signals
- Be aware of your own body language
- Respect other people's personal space
- Watch your image

$\boxed{2}$ Getting Off to a Good Start

In this chapter:
- Why is it important?
- Approaching other people who are:
  - on their own
  - in a group
- Other people approaching you who are:
  - angry
  - in a hurry
  - senior to you
  - on your level
  - junior to you
  - strangers

■ Why is it important?

Getting a conversation off to a good start is important because it sets the tone of the whole meeting. If you get off on the wrong foot with someone, there are likely to be misunderstandings, ill feeling and even anger and aggression. Then you both have to spend time and energy back-tracking, breaking down the barriers, building bridges and starting again.

Things can go wrong as the conversation goes along, but if you have got it off to a good start, this is less likely to happen.

Much of what happens is in your control – how you present yourself, how you start a conversation off or how you react to other people. The first part of this chapter is about how you approach other people, and the second part is about how you can deal with people who are approaching you in different ways.

Authors' note

In this chapter we are often talking about you and one other person. To say his/her, him/her all the time is awkward. The authors have, therefore, decided to use 'their' and 'them' when referring to one person, although strictly speaking this is not correct.

 # Approaching other people who are on their own

When you are going up to someone, whether that someone is standing or sitting, remember that you are entering their territory. Here are some points to bear in mind:

- Approach from the front if you are able to do so, so that they can see you coming and can prepare themselves to meet you.
- If they are busy, or concentrating, try not to barge in or interrupt. Wait for a fraction of a second to be acknowledged – a wave of the hand, a smile, a nod, eye contact, is enough. If you are junior to or are on the same level as the person you are approaching, you would automatically respect their right to be busy doing something else and would wait for them to acknowledge you. If you are senior to someone, is there any reason why you should not do the same thing?
- Do not lean on their desk or table uninvited especially if this means leaning over them. Be careful about putting a hand on their shoulder – respect their personal space.
- If you have something to give them (papers, for example) do not fling them on the desk or thrust them into their hand. Offer them so that the other person can accept them; offer them the right way round so that the other person can immediately read them.
- If the matter is urgent, or you are in a hurry, your body language will probably convey this. If it does not, say that you have not got much time. Most people tend to think that their business is more important or urgent than anybody else's, but it is usually not so. When it is, say so.
- If you are cross or angry, try to calm down before approaching someone. Things are much more likely to go well if you are in control of yourself. Shouting at someone might make you feel good for a while, but in the end you will have to sort the matter out in a

sensible sort of way, which will be much more difficult if you have started off by antagonising the other person or making them feel small.

If all this sounds a bit unnatural or unnecessary, try it and see what happens. Try it on someone you don't get on with very well – it may not succeed the first time, but in the end it probably will.

 ## Approaching other people who are in a group

Do you remember, as a child, barging into a room full of something you wanted to say, and one of the adults saying, "Just a minute, I'm talking"?

If you do the same thing now, the people in the group will probably not tell you not to interrupt, but they will certainly convey it by their body language – frowning, turning away a little, not opening the group to let you become part of it. Watch their feet! If you are welcome, their feet will turn out to meet you. If you are not, only people's bodies will turn.

You will be conveying by your own body language whether what you have to say is urgent or exciting, or whether you just want to be part of the group. Here are a few points to consider:

- Approach the group, whether they are standing or sitting, where there is a little gap.
- Hover on the edge of the group for a moment, and wait to be acknowledged.
- When someone smiles at you, or moves to let you join in, move into the group.
- Do not immediately chime in with your opinion – you will probably get it wrong if you have not heard the whole story. If you have something important to say, the others will soon get the message and you will be the centre of attention.

What we have said here is only a matter of common courtesy and good sense, but many people forget these things in the heat of the moment, and make it difficult for other people to accept them or listen to what they have to say. Acceptance depends quite a lot on how you present yourself in the first place.

Practice – What would you do next?

In these scenarios it is up to you to make the next move.

- You have to take some papers to a junior manager sitting in her office. The door is open, she is busy on the phone with her back to you. You need to give a short word of explanation with the papers. She does not turn round. You are in a hurry. What would you do next?
- You are very excited about something and dying to share it with someone. You rush up to your colleague or friend who is reading something which is obviously upsetting. What would you do next?
- There is a group of people having a very absorbing conversation. You do not know any of them very well, but have a message for one of them. What would you do next?

Other people approaching you

In the second part of this chapter we shall be considering how to deal with people who approach you in various ways. A few lines of explanation describe the situation and the table then shows what you could do in each case to get the conversation off to a good start – or as good as it can reasonably be. In many cases you will not be the first to speak and you will be relying on your body language to steer your side of the conversation.

- *You are on your own concentrating on what you are doing, or perhaps on the phone. Someone comes storming up to you, obviously very ANGRY – you have no idea why.*

ACKNOWLEDGE	Show quickly that you know the person is there. Do not smile or say hello, good morning etc.
STOP WHAT YOU ARE DOING	Do this as quickly as possible. If you are on the phone, offer to ring the person back, if possible.

24

BODY LANGUAGE	If you are sitting down, stay sitting and let the other person talk. To get up at once looks confrontational, and they need to dominate for a while. Sit still and upright; if you lean forward it might took aggressive.
	If you are standing, turn your whole body to face that person, but do not get too close, which looks confrontational. Stand your ground calmly. Do not turn away nor back away.
	Do not look closed or aggressive. Maintain eye contact and look attentive.
	Show that you are listening by giving little nods.
	Let the person run out of steam. Only when the angry person has calmed down will you be able to discuss the matter sensibly together.

• *You are in the same situation. The person approaching you is obviously IN A HURRY.*

ACKNOWLEDGE	Look up, smile, say or answer 'hello' etc.
STOP WHAT YOU ARE DOING	Stop as soon as you are able. If you are on the phone, offer to ring back, if possible.
BODY LANGUAGE	Look brisk; give the person your whole attention, turning your whole body and head towards them; maintain eye contact and lean forward slightly, which shows that you are interested.
	If you are sitting behind a desk or table, stay where you are unless you need to look at something together.

• *This time the person coming to talk to you is SENIOR TO YOU.*

| ACKNOWLEDGE | Look up, smile and say good morning etc. |
| STOP WHAT YOU ARE DOING | Stop as soon as possible. Offer to ring back, if necessary. |

BODY LANGUAGE	Give the person your whole attention.
	If you are sitting down, stand up if it is customary to do so. Offer them a seat, if appropriate, and sit down again yourself. If you are standing and they are sitting, you will appear to dominate.
	If you are standing, turn your whole body to the person, but do not go too close. Let them come to you if they wish.
	Tilt your head to one side to show that you are listening. Lean forward a little to show that you are interested.
	Turn papers, screen etc towards them if required.

- *A FRIEND OR COLLEAGUE comes to you, in no particular hurry.*

ACKNOWLEDGE	Look up, smile, wave them to a chair, if appropriate.
STOP WHAT YOU ARE DOING	Carry on until you come to a natural break in what you are doing. Apologise for keeping them waiting.
BODY LANGUAGE	Open, friendly, interested. No need to move.

- *Someone JUNIOR TO YOU comes to see you.*

ACKNOWLEDGE	Look up, greet them with a smile, invite them to sit down, if appropriate.
STOP WHAT YOU ARE DOING	When you come to a natural break, stop what you are doing and invite the person to talk.
BODY LANGUAGE	Sit or stand looking attentive, giving occasional nods. Look at them, not beyond them.
	Beware of looking too laid-back or arrogant. Show you have got time for what they have to say.
	If there is a deadline, say so and arrange another meeting if necessary.

• A STRANGER, *expected or unexpected comes to see you.*

ACKNOWLEDGE	Look up, smile, indicate a chair, if appropriate.
STOP WHAT YOU ARE DOING	Do this immediately, if possible. If you are on the phone offer to ring back. Apologise for keeping the person waiting.
BODY LANGUAGE	Go to the person, shake hands. Invite them to sit down, or sit down again. Sit down yourself with no barriers (desks etc) between you. Arrange your chair at an angle, and try to sit in a chair on the same level as your visitor's. Pass the time of day; arrange refreshments, if appropriate, before getting down to business.

As you will see from the charts, you should always acknowledge someone, stop what you are doing as soon as you reasonably can and make sure your body language is appropriate to the situation. People often fail to acknowledge the presence of the person quickly enough, which is almost bound to get the conversation off to a bad start.

The self-presentation skills you use can make a lot of difference to the way a conversation goes. Be aware of what you do now, and if necessary plan to make improvements. In the meantime, say what you would do in the following situations.

☐ *Practice – what would you do next?*

In each situation, the next move is up to you.
• You are sitting working, really concentrating. You feel, rather than see, someone just behind you, wanting something, but not wanting to distract you. What would you do next?
• You are standing watching something or someone; it is very important that you do not take your eyes off that person or that thing for an instant (perhaps it is a shoplifter). Someone rushes up to you with an urgent, written message from your manager. What would you do next?

- You are sitting talking to someone on the telephone; it is not a conversation it would be easy to end abruptly. Your manager, who is a cold fish, comes up to you purposefully, obviously angry. He is not the sort of person who shouts and he is too well-mannered to interrupt. He stands looking at you and waiting. What would you do next?

Points to remember from this chapter

- Things are more likely to go well if they get off to a good start. The way you use your self presentation skills influences this
- Approach one person from the front, don't interrupt, don't throw or thrust papers at them
- Approach a group through a gap, don't burst in, wait to be acknowledged, join the group
Use your skills to adapt to the way in which people approach you:
  - acknowledge their presence
  - stop what you are doing
  - use the appropriate body language and words

3 Oral Assessment

In this chapter:
- The importance of oral assessment
- The range of activities assessed
- What do assessors look for?

 ## The importance of oral assessment

How well can you communicate verbally? That is what this chapter is all about. Effective verbal communication is important in so many different aspects of life: work, social, formal, informal and so on. This is why the assessment of your ability to communicate verbally is now an integral part of many exams, integrated schemes and profiles.

You will notice that this chapter is called 'Oral Assessment' not 'How to Perform in an Oral Examination'. This is because you are likely to be assessed in a great variety of situations; oral assessments are no longer just a question of attending an interview and answering questions about a passage you have just read, or giving your opinion on a prepared topic. Some oral assessments are carried out in the 'interview' situation, but many are not, and you need to be able to communicate successfully in many different environments.

This chapter is mainly concerned with your ability to communicate verbally in English, but much of what is said here applies equally to oral examinations in foreign languages. Assessors or examiners are not interested in how well you can repeat facts that you have learnt; they are much more interested in how well you can express your opinions, how logically you can put forward your point of view and how well you interact with others. In oral examinations in a foreign language, you will also be assessed on your ability to convey your thoughts with reasonably correct grammar and an understandable accent, but these are technical aspects which are not the subject of this chapter.

28

This chapter is about the ability to intereact and communicate with others, verbally, in a variety of situations.

The range of activities assessed

It depends which exam or integrated scheme you are involved in; you need to know and be quite clear about the situations in which you are likely to be assessed. You might be involved in one or several of the following:

● **Small group discussion – member**
You are a member of a small (4–6 people) discussion group. You will be assessed on your ability to interact with the other members of the group and put forward your own point of view (see Chapter 9 – In a Formal Meeting, for guidance).

● **Small group discussion – leader**
You are the leader or Chair of a small (4–6 people) discussion group. You will be assessed on your ability to introduce the topic to be discussed and to chair the meeting (see Chapter 10 – Chairing a Discussion Group, for guidance).

● **Group discussion from a given source**
Your group is discussing, perhaps, a video, a film, a book, a play, etc. You will be assessed on your ability to put forward your opinions or your impressions of the topic of conversation.

● **A formal debate**
You are proposing or seconding, opposing or seconding a very definite standpoint. For example, you might be asked to propose or oppose the motion 'This house (this group) is for/against capital punishment'. You will be assessed on your ability to get your thoughts together in a logical way and put across a persuasive argument.

● **Role play**
You take part in a role play to illustrate a particular situation – perhaps a complaining customer and how to handle such a person. You are not assessed on your acting ability, but on the way in which you, as a person, would handle the situation being enacted.

● **Reading aloud and/or play reading**
You are reading aloud a passage from a book, or reading a character in a play. You are assessed on your ability to read fluently and with expression, and in the case of play reading, to give your character some realism.

● **Individual talk on a prepared topic to a group**
You stand up in front of a group and make a prepared presentation.
You are assessed on your ability to get your thoughts together and,
with the use of visual aids if appropriate, present your topic to the
group in an effective way (see Chapter 11 – In Front of a Group of
People, for guidance).

● **Individual conversations**
You are involved in a conversation with one other person. You are
assessed on your ability to listen, respond and put forward your own
point of view so that the conversation has a good two-way flow
without too much emotion creeping in.

● **Giving instructions**
You have to give someone else instructions on how to do something
or how to get somewhere. You are assessed on your ability to tell
someone clearly and accurately what they need to know: the ultimate
proof of your ability to communicate in this area is whether the other
person can actually do the task or arrive at the right place (see
Chapter 8 – Showing Someone How to do Something, for guidance).

● **Reporting back**
You have to report back to your own group, or your 'boss' on
something you have seen and heard or in which you have
participated (a meeting, for example). You are assessed on how fully
you report back in a logical and unbiased sort of way.

● **Describing something**
You have to describe something you have seen or heard – for
example, a fashion show, a speech or a TV current affairs programme.
You are assessed on how well you can make the description 'live' for
the people who are listening to you. Can they, at secondhand, hear
and/or see what you are describing?

● **Giving an account of what you have learnt**
You have recently learnt something on a course, or in a class, and are
telling your listeners what it is you have learnt. You are assessed on
the clarity with which you can explain to your listeners what it is
you have recently learnt.

● **Answering questions in an interview/exam**
You are asked questions about a topic you have studied or a piece
you have just read. You are assessed on your knowledge of the topic
or your understanding of the piece you have read and your ability to
express what you have understood.

You will see from all these situations that you are being assessed on
how well you interact with other people and are able to put forward
your own point of view. Later in this chapter we shall be looking at
the abilities you need to display and what assessors are looking for.

For now, identify which of these situations you are likely to encounter in your oral assessment.

Practice 1

- Make a list (it might only be one item) of the situations in which you are likely to find yourself for an oral assessment. Will they be group work, informal conversations, formal presentations, interviews or what? If you do not know, it is important to find out from your teacher, lecturer, tutor or trainer which of the assessment situations you will be involved in. If you do not know what you are letting yourself in for, it is much more difficult to prepare.
- Having identified the situations, write alongside each one a broad description of what your assessor or examiner will be looking for. For example:
  LEADING A DISCUSSION – ability to introduce the subject and control the discussion so that everyone is able to say what they want to.
- You might find it helpful to draw up a table of the situations and the broad assessment points at this stage. As you work through the following sections, you will be able to add more detail about what abilities you need, what an assessor is looking for and what your own strengths and weaknesses are.

  Your table could look something like the example on the next page, and will probably need to be landscape (across a wide page).

What do assessors look for?

There are three main abilities you need to display when communicating verbally with others:
- Listening
- Speaking
- Interacting

Of course these three elements are the basis of all good verbal communication, so they are mentioned frequently in this book. Being

Self Assessment Table

Situation	Assessment Points	Personal Weaknesses	Personal Strengths
Discussion group member	• Interaction with others • Put forward own viewpoint • Listening		
Discussion group leader	• Introduce subject • Control discussion • Listening		
Prepared talk	• Preparation • Visual aids • Clarity • Audience interest		

assessed on your competence in these areas adds an extra dimension – you need to show that you are indeed competent, without going over the top.

How can you show an assessor or examiner what your abilities are? What does an assessor look for?

Listening

An assessor will be watching you to see how well you listen. If you are in a discussion group and looking laid-back with your eyes closed, you might well be listening very intently, but you do not look as though you are.

Look at the person who is speaking – turn your body and your chair, if necessary, as well as your head. Maintain eye contact with the speaker, and lean forward, giving the occasional nod to show that you are interested and understand what is being said.

If you do not understand, that is no disgrace – it might be that the speaker has not put the point or asked the question clearly. Ask questions yourself to clarify what has been said: this will show you are listening with intelligence.

Sometimes it is possible to look as though you are listening, when in fact your mind has gone off in quite another direction. Listening is a very active thing to do, and requires real concentration. If you have not been listening well, it will soon become obvious when it is your turn to speak. This sort of thing can happen in conversation, in discussion groups and also in a formal presentation situation when your audience is asking questions of you, invited or not.

Speaking

When it is your turn to speak, what are assessors looking for? Above all they are looking for clarity – clarity of thought and speech.

Have you got all your thoughts together in a sensible, logical way, particularly if you have had a chance to prepare what you are going to say? If you dodge from one topic to another and backtrack on yourself, the listeners and the assessor will find it very hard to understand what you are talking about. (See Chapter 8 – Showing Someone How to do Something, and Chapter 11 – In Front of a Group of People, for guidance on how to get your thoughts together so that you can show others how clear your thinking is.)

Your speech itself also needs to be clear. It has to be loud enough for everyone to hear and clear enough for everyone to understand. This does not mean that you have to speak with what is called 'received pronunciation' (RP), a sort of standard, southern or BBC English. Your dialect is quite acceptable, provided that what you are saying is clear.

What about the words you use? Here again, an assessor will not be looking for perfect grammar. It is important when you are writing that your grammar is right, so that other people understand what you have written. When you are speaking, it is acceptable to use the expressions and phrases you would normally use and are comfortable with, provided your listeners understand what you are saying. It is better not to try to use more upmarket phrases and words, if you would not normally do so – they will probably sound false and forced to you and your listeners. On the other hand swearing is not acceptable, and it is better not to use too many slang words or local dialect words. Consider your listeners, and use words and phrases you are comfortable with and which they will understand.

What if you have a speech impediment – anything from a lisp to a stammer? This does not mean that an assessor will mark you down. Assessors normally bend over backwards to give you all the credit they can; provided you can show that you have listened and understood and can make your points in a way which others can understand, there is no reason to fear oral assessment.

Interacting

Here we are talking about how you relate to others, what sort of image you present and generally how you come across.

For example, in a discussion group, do you dominate the whole proceedings and talk too much? If so, you are probably not listening very well, and will be marked down accordingly. On the other hand, are you one of those people who sit and stand looking thoroughly bored and closed (see Chapter 1 – Body Language)? You may not feel like that inside, but that is the impression you can sometimes give without meaning to, particularly if you are shy. Quiet people should never be underestimated, and assessors will not mark you down just because you are quiet, but they can hardly give you marks for speaking well or interacting well with others if you sit looking down and not saying anything.

What about your appearance? If your oral assessment is a formal exam, it is wise to wear something which looks reasonably formal. This does not mean that you necessarily have to wear a suit if you are not used to wearing one, but torn jeans and sloppy sweaters do not give a very good impression. Assessors are human, and will tend to give good marks to people who look clean, neat and alert –

bright-eyed and bushy-tailed, in fact. Think about your appearance and make sure it is suitable for the occasion.

Some people always look good, no matter what they wear. Some people find it very difficult to look good, even if the clothes themselves are fashionable and well-made. If you are one of those people, at least you can be sure to look clean and well-pressed, including shoes, hair, nails, skirt, trousers and so on.

Practice 2

- Practise your listening skills: listen to ten minutes of a television or radio programme, and see if, when it has finished, you can write down in two or three sentences what it was about. This will also help you practise your reporting back.
- Read what you have written aloud to yourself, and record it on cassette. Play it back and see what you sound like – is your voice clear and easy to listen to?
- Leave the machine on RECORD while you are talking to someone else until you have forgotten that the tape is on. (You should warn the other person that you are going to do this, and explain it is for you to hear what *you* sound like.) It might take quite a long time to forget the tape is running, but if you can manage to do it and play the tape back later, you will hear what you *really* sound like. It can come as quite a shock. It will also show you how you interact with others, and whether you are too dominant or too quiet.
- Analyse your own strengths and weaknesses and add them to your chart. If you need to improve your listening and speaking skills, at least you will know how good you are and where exactly improvement is needed.

If you can remember that assessors and examiners are not out to trap you, but want to give you as much credit as they can, it will help you to show yourself at your best, and that is what they are looking for.

Points to remember from this chapter

- What sort of situation(s) will you be in while you are being assessed?
- What will assessors be looking for in those situations?
- Do you need to prepare anything specific?
- What will you wear?
- How good are you at listening?
- How good are you at putting your thoughts together in a clear and logical way?
- How good are you at expressing yourself?
- How well do you relate to and interact with others?
- What is your body language like in these situations?
- In what areas do you need to improve?
- How are you going to do this?

4 At a Job Interview

In this chapter:
- Job interviews
- First impressions
- Attitude
- Clear thinking
- Speech
- Body language
- Mannerisms
- Conversation piece
- Last impressions

Job interviews

Imagine that you have already completed the Application Form, and sent it off with your CV and covering letter. You have made sure you have come to the correct address, and that your arrival is known to the right person by the appointed time. We take up the story from where you are about to come face-to-face with your interviewer.

Whether this is your first important job interview, or whether you are a seasoned interviewee – for whatever reason – it is worth reminding yourself of some of the basics for a successful interview; successful in the sense that you are offered the job you are applying for.

First impressions

Whatever training your interviewer may have had about being objective in dealing with interviewees, and however much (s)he

attempts to put it into practice, make no mistake about it, the image
you present to your interviewer as you walk through the door of the
interview room will create an impression on the interviewer which
might be difficult to shift – even if, during the course of the
interview, you turn out to be a different type of person.

First impressions linger. Think of your own experiences of
meeting people for the first time; however well you get to know
them later, something of that initial image will remain with you.

It is a sobering thought that the whole course of a person's life
could be changed by an impression given to somebody else when
walking into a room.

So, what does all this mean to an interviewee? It means that you
need to think carefully about how you are going to appear to your
interviewer. Appearance is not only about clothes, although they play
a large part, of course. Equally important is how you yourself appear.
For example, does your hair look clean and well-groomed? Are your
face and hands clean? Are your finger nails of a suitable length, with
no dirt lurking under them? If you wear nail varnish, is it of a
suitable colour, and unchipped? If you smoke, have you made sure
that your fingers are not stained with nicotine? If you are applying
for a job in an office you may consider that nicotine-stained fingers
do not matter, but your prospective employer could well think
otherwise. On the other hand if you are likely to be working among
heavy machinery on a factory floor, the state of your fingers really
might not matter. If you will be handling food, particularly open
food, or showing customers high-quality and expensive items of
stock, unsightly nicotine-stained fingers would matter a great deal.

Fairly formal clothes are usually best for an interview, but casual
clothes can sometimes be appropriate. Either way they should be
clean and smart. Think about the organisation from your
interviewer's point of view. What type of business is it? What sort of
job are you being interviewed for? If you were the interviewer, and
representing that business, what type of person would you want to
see walking through your door? Probably somebody you could see
fitting in with the job situation and the company image – remember
what an effect that first impression has.

Attitude

A basic requirement is that you appear to be interested in the job.
That statement is not quite as silly as it sounds. A lot will depend on

how you came to be at the interview. If you have come there through
your own initiative, by replying to an advertisement, filling in the
application form and doing your background research, you will
automatically have a positive attitude, because you will want a
successful outcome to all your efforts. On the other hand if you have
just been sent along by the Job Centre or an employment agency
without being properly briefed about what job you are going for,
you might feel confused. This could come over to your interviewer as
not being interested; an obvious death knell for the outcome of the
interview.

Your attitude about yourself needs to be positive. Even if your
experience of a particular subject area is limited, refer to it in a
positive way; remember you have an advantage over another
applicant who might not have had any experience at all in that
subject.

Clear thinking

The ability to think clearly in an interview comes from careful
preparation and doing your homework. This should cover subjects
such as the company, its products and/or services, its competitors, its
way of doing business, its background/history.

Take your time when answering questions, do not be pressured
into making hurried statements, particularly when you have some
important points to make, perhaps about particular experience you
have or qualifications you have achieved.

Using your own first-hand experience to illustrate your points
will help you to think clearly about what you are saying. Be honest
and straightforward, do not flannel or over-elaborate, you might get
caught out!

If you really do not know the answer to a question, say so but do
not do it too often. If a question is not clear, do not ask the
interviewer to repeat it, but say something like 'Did you mean
so-and-so?'. This will make the interviewer put the question again in
a different way, and you stand more chance of understanding it. This
is particularly useful when you are trying to answer complicated
questions – it gives you time to think, too.

Speech

When you are giving information and answering questions, think about *how* you are doing it. Apart from the fact of not talking too loudly or too quietly or quickly, make sure that you can be clearly understood by your interviewer. This does not mean that you should try to speak with a posh accent, or one that is not your own. It does mean that you should try to speak clearly, without mumbling. Look straight at your interviewer, not down at your hands or elsewhere in the room – it will help the communication between you.

Will the job you are applying for involve you in speaking to others, either directly or by telephone, as a significant part of your daily routine? For example, if your job will involve your talking to customers, the clarity of your speech could be a key element in the job, and the interviewer will be paying particular attention to the way in which your voice comes over at the interview.

Body language

You present a picture of yourself to your interviewer by the way you walk into and out of the interview room, and the way you sit in your chair. Remind yourself of the various 'messages' which posture – particularly when adopted unconsciously – can send to your interviewer by looking at the chapter on Body Language at the beginning of this book. For example, be careful about waving your arms about, or sitting with your legs in an ungainly manner.

Clothes help your image. If you are wearing casual clothes, you tend to move and sit in a casual way. In more formal dress, because of its cut for one thing, you unconsciously move and sit in a more formal manner. This could present a more business-like image to your interviewer. Once again, if the job you are applying for will involve you in being before the public, the image you present at your interview could be significant.

It could be a good idea, prior to the interview, to practise getting rid of any 'props' (personal possessions) you may have with you, because you will want to go into the interview room in as natural a way as possible. For example, if you are carrying a briefcase, a handbag (or both), an umbrella or a coat, think what you are going to do with them when you are asked by your interviewer to sit down.

Your aim must be to be 'sitting comfortably', so that you can concentrate wholly on the interview, and not be distracted by bags, coats or brollies.

The key is to act as calmly and as smoothly as possible. Take your time, and show that you are in control of your actions; it will also give you that little moment to settle yourself down and get your mind round to the matter in hand – presenting a favourable impression of yourself.

Ask where you should put your coat or umbrella, if you have not been able to leave these articles outside. Put your bag or briefcase on the floor. Try to avoid arriving with belongings in a plastic bag; it does not look very business-like.

Practise dealing with all these things and sitting comfortably in a chair at home, so that when you get to the interview, it all happens naturally.

Mannerisms

Mannerisms are defined in the dictionary as 'affected gestures or habits and/or manners of speaking etc' – try to avoid them. Mannerisms are those little habits we often do not realise that we are doing or saying. For that reason they can be distracting to an interviewer. Mannerisms can often be exaggerated through nervousness or apprehension. Try to establish what your current ones are, and be aware of when you are using them. Perhaps a friend you trust could help you.

Physical mannerisms could be things like: playing with your fingers, touching your mouth or hair, rubbing your eyes, fidgeting, crossing and uncrossing your legs, shifting your feet on the floor. Watch other people and see what theirs are.

Some verbal mannerisms tend to go in fashions. For example, 'unbelievable', 'you know', adding 'like' at the end of a sentence, 'dunno', 'that's about it'. Others are signs of nervousness, like 'um' and 'er'.

Do not feel that you have to 'sit to attention' all the time in case you make a distracting movement. Do not feel, either, that you have to answer questions without elaboration in case you say something out of place. Try to be as natural as possible. Be yourself, but at the same time be alert to the visual and verbal image and impression you are presenting to your interviewer.

Conversation piece

A good interview should be a conversation between two people – the giving and receiving of information by both parties. For each there will be a time to speak and a time to listen.

From the interviewee's point of view, once you have said 'good morning' or 'good afternoon', and settled yourself down, wait until the interviewer obviously wants you to speak. It is not a good idea to take over the early stages of the interview, when the lead will be taken by the interviewer. It is important to listen when questions are being put to you, so that you can understand precisely what is being asked. If you do not understand the questions you will not be able to put your own point of view in a sensible way. If you know that you have strengths, do not be afraid to tell the interviewer about them. If you know that you have weaknesses, do not be afraid to acknowledge them, but say that you are confident you can improve with help or training.

Throughout the interview try to show enthusiasm and sincerity. Insincerity will show through if you do not genuinely believe in what you are saying, or you are simply trying to make an impression for the sake of what you think your interviewer expects to hear from you. Be natural, be yourself, be sincere. Keep your end of the conversation going, but do not interrupt when the interviewer is talking. Listen, and show that you are listening.

Towards the end of the interview that awkward moment arrives when the interviewer asks 'Do you want to ask me anything?', and your mind goes blank. Avoid this situation becoming embarrassing, for both of you, by having some questions thought out in advance. Write them on a piece of paper or your note pad and refer to them before responding to the interviewer. Apart from giving you something to say, your interviewer could (or should) be impressed by the fact that you have done this bit of thoughtful preparation.

Ask questions about the company or the responsibilities of the job rather than about salary or holidays. If you do not know what the conditions of employment will be, you have every right to ask, but mix these questions in with questions which show you are interested in the job. If you have important dates already booked, eg holiday dates, it is as well to say so at the interview stage rather than start work and immediately ask for time off.

By the end of the conversation both you and your interviewer should know as much as you need to carry on to the next stage of the selection process, but the interview is not quite over yet.

Last impressions

Your exit from an interview is as important as your entrance.
However well or badly you feel the interview has gone, show
courtesy to your interviewer, collect your belongings together in the
same controlled way as you disposed of them on arrival, and leave
the interview room in a confident manner. Remember to thank others
who have been involved in any way during your visit – the person
who greeted you on arrival, the one who maybe provided you with
some refreshment while you were waiting. Sometimes these people
are asked by an interviewer for an assessment of your behaviour
outside the interview room, so it is useful to bear in mind that your
interview could last from the moment you enter the premises to the
time you leave the building or the car park. If you go to an interview
in your car, it might be an idea to give that a wash and brush up, as
well as the attention you are going to give to your own personal
appearance.

So, having made a good impression at the start, you finish by
leaving your interviewer convinced that you are the right person for
the job: your attention to detail could have given you the edge over
the competition.

Practice

It is difficult to practise job interviews, except in a role play
situation, but there are things you can do:
- Review your wardrobe, and make sure you have suitable
  'interview' clothes.
- Find out about the types of business or organisation to which
  you think you will apply for a job.
- Listen to the way you talk – use a cassette player as suggested
  in Chapter 3 – Oral Assessment. A job interview is really only
  another form of oral assessment.
- Practise sitting confidently, so you know what to do with your
  arms, hands, legs, bags and so on. Chapter 1 – Body Language,
  will help.
- Before each interview check through the list of Points to
  remember which follows.

Points to remember from this chapter

- First impressions linger
- Are you dressed suitably?
- Be positive
- Do your homework about the company
- Answer questions clearly – take your time
- Sit confidently, but not too laid-back
- Avoid physical and verbal mannerisms
- An interview is a conversation: listen to the interviewer and respond fully and honestly
- Write down in advance questions you want to ask
- An interview can last from the time you arrive at the venue to the moment you leave

5 On the Telephone

In this chapter:
CALLER
- Think clearly
- Arrange logically
- Express clearly
- Use understandable language
- Give details concisely

RECEIVER
- Message taking
- Answering
- Listening
- Transferring calls
- Misunderstandings
- Irate callers
- Saying no
- Hanging on

ANSWERING MACHINES
- Talking to machines
- Machine owners

 ## Caller

How often do you pick up the telephone without really thinking through beforehand what you want to say? That can be a wasteful and expensive exercise, for you, if it is your telephone, or your employer, if you are at work. The key to a successful call will be – as so often in matters of effective communication – good preparation. As you can see, being a telephone caller carries its own responsibilities.

What sort of calls do you normally have to make, either at work or in your social life? Think about how you go about making a telephone call. Do you just pick up the handset, dial or key in the number and get on with it? Do you pause a moment before doing that and ask yourself why you are making the call? Are you clear about the objective of the call, and what you want to gain from the conversation (not a monologue from you or your receiver)?

Consider these five stages to making effective telephone calls as the caller:
- Think clearly
- Arrange logically
- Express clearly
- Use understandable language
- Give details concisely

Think clearly

Here is a checklist to help you to think clearly before making a call:
- Know exactly *what* you have to ask or say before dialling or keying in the number
- Know *who* you want to speak to:
  – Who is the right person to receive your call? Do you have an extension number or other means of identity to save time in making direct contact?
  If you do not know who you should speak to:
  – Say what you are calling about; the person answering will be able to say whether you have got through to the right extension
- Know *why* you are *telephoning* that person – as opposed to sending a letter, a memo or a fax
- Establish in your own mind what information you want from your receiver, or what action you want taken when your call is over. You can then aim the content of the call towards those goals
- Think of the best time to ring – for the receiver. Is it likely to be more convenient for your receiver to handle your call at one time of the day rather than at another? Is the time governed by the action *you* need to take as a result of the call? Can you make the call – and can your receiver take it – just as easily during the time when cheaper rates apply?

Arrange logically

Try to break down the main purpose or subject of your call into a logical sequence, to provide a framework for your conversation. Just writing down a checklist of headings, or relevant figures or dates will probably be sufficient to make sure you do not miss out anything vital. It can be very embarrassing to have to call back as soon as you have replaced the handset, simply because you have remembered something important you meant to say. So, make sure you have all the information you need for your call ready-to-hand by the telephone.

There could, of course, be more than one logical sequence. Choose the one which you think will suit your receiver, or which will help you achieve the objective of your call. This is easier if you know your receiver. If you are not acquainted, put yourself in the receiver's place and try to think of the most suitable sequence for *receiving* your information.

It is a useful idea to plan your opening statement, particularly if you are broaching a new, or tricky, subject. Do not write an essay, just something to help you get over the initial hurdle of introducing yourself and the subject of your call.

Asking yourself these sorts of questions might help:
- what knowledge does the receiver have, or is likely to have, of the subject I want to raise?
- how can I best lead from my opening statement into the main purpose of the call?
- how can I get the receiver interested in the subject and purpose of my call?
- which are the essential points I want to emphasise?

Express clearly

When communicating with the spoken word, a clear, strong – though not overpowering – voice is necessary. In spite of your preparation for the call, the ability to 'think on your feet' and form accurate sentences while you are speaking is very useful, and something worth practising.

Your knowledge of what you are talking about, plus the preparation you have done before your call, should help your fluency.

Hesitations, erms and ahs will not only reduce the speed at which you are communicating *effectively*, they will also cause irritation and break your receiver's concentration.

In any case it is a good idea to give the receiver time to 'tune in' to who you are and why you are ringing, especially if you are making contact for the first time. If you know your receiver, all you need to do is make a few chatty remarks, but do not get bogged down in irrelevancies at the expense of getting on with the main reason for your call.

Speaking directly into the mouthpiece is a great aid to clarity. Some people manage to dangle it under their chins, and then wonder why they cannot be heard. Try to avoid those lazy habits, which you can get away with in face-to-face conversation, like mumbling, dropping the voice at the end of a sentence or slurring words together. Remember your voice is your only means of contact; make sure that it does a good job on your behalf. Chapter 3 – Oral Assessment goes into detail about clarity of speech, accents etc.

Some people are nervous about talking on the telephone, and nervousness can lead to gabbling, which is very confusing and off-putting for the receiver. So, if you are feeling a little apprehensive about a particular call, start slowly, until you get into your stride, and then try to vary your pace according to what you have to say. The way you stand or sit can make a difference, as well. If you want to sound authoritative, try standing up to make your call. If you are feeling nervous, sit straight but relaxed; it will help you with your breathing and prevent the nervousness in your voice being too apparent at the other end.

Having thought about what you want to say in advance will help you give the right emphasis to the important points. Try to pause after you have made an important point or statement, to allow your receiver to take in the significance of what you have just said.

Try not to shout down the telephone, or go to the other extreme, so that your receiver has difficulty in making out what you are saying. A warm, friendly voice will always tend to hold the attention of a receiver, rather than a brusque, offhand one. Try smiling down the telephone; you will find it does wonders because it lifts the muscles in your cheeks, and makes quite a difference to your tone of voice.

Visualise the person you are talking to, even if you have never met him or her. It helps to make the call more personal.

Do not overlook the use of questions in a telephone conversation to gather information, to help establish understanding between you and your receiver, or to highlight any areas which need to be clarified. Use open questions, which start with words like 'what', 'why', 'where', 'when', 'how' and 'who', if you want the receiver to clarify something or give you specific information. Asking 'How often will you be able to contact me?' will winkle out much more information then asking 'Will you be able to contact me?', to which the receiver could reply merely 'Yes' or 'No'.

Use understandable language

Try always to keep in mind the knowledge your receiver has of the subject you are discussing. If it is likely to be an area new to the receiver, beware of using jargon terms, or, if you must, make sure you explain them. On the other hand, do not start explaining terms to someone who is well-acquainted with the subject matter, or you could find yourself on the losing end of your call. Perhaps the well-known communication principle, Keep It Short and Simple (KISS) could be a good convention to follow.

Convey a sincere interest and conviction in what you are saying. Certain tones of voice, especially those conveying irony and humour, seem to get lost in transit. Jokes can misfire and flippancies can easily be taken as serious comment – sometimes with disastrous results. It is usually best to keep the lighthearted stuff until you are talking to your receiver face-to-face, when the extra element of being there in person will help to underline that your statements are not meant to be taken too seriously.

It is desirable to check back with your receiver on all vital information before finishing the call. Things like telephone numbers, names, addresses or product details are all worth reading back, to make certain that you both have the same – and correct – information.

Give details concisely

Be as concise as you can: that means saying things in a short, logical sort of way. However, do not be so concise that what you are saying becomes unclear to your receiver.

Remember, though, that time is money as far as telephone calls are concerned, and try to use the time you are actually connected with your receiver to further the purpose of your call. Although the time is ticking by, and the cost adding up, you must appear calm and assured to your receiver. Your preparation will help you to make sure that every second counts, and that the objective of your call is achieved in the most economical time possible, consistent with courtesy and resolution.

Perhaps all this sounds rather uninteresting and clinical, but you can use it as a framework for your own personality. You can be pleasant and good to listen to on the telephone, so that people are glad that you have called, but unless you plan and make your calls in a businesslike way, the people you call will finally get frustrated.

Receiver

Being the receiver of telephone calls also carries certain
responsibilities. One of the most basic is always to have a pen or
pencil by the telephone. Have it attached to the desk or wall by a
piece of string, if necessary; anything to make sure there is always
something readily available to write down information arriving by
telephone.

Message taking

How do you take down telephone messages or information at home
or at work? Do you use the first scrap of paper that comes to hand?
Do you write on paper bags meant to wrap customers' purchases? Do
you perhaps write on the wall above the telephone? The answer is
very simple: *always* have a proper message pad by the telephone, to
be used for no other purpose than to write down telephone
messages. Have a proper system of ensuring that as one pad is used
up so it is replaced with a new one.

What do you do with the message or information once it *is*
written down? Have a definite place where you put the written
messages until you pass them on.

Answering

When the telephone rings, do you take a breath before answering,
particularly if you are in the middle of doing something else? Doing
this simple exercise will help to give you a calmer voice as you
speak.

Do you answer the telephone while still speaking to someone
else? Don't: the caller will think that you are not interested in the
call.

How do you answer and identify yourself to your caller? If you
are at work, give a greeting first (good morning, good afternoon etc)
and then say the name of the company, department etc followed by
your own name. This gives your caller time to tune in to your voice.
If you are at home, your own number followed by a greeting could
be sufficient. Just saying 'hallo' does not really do much for your
caller, even on an ordinary domestic call.

Listening

Do you actively listen to what the caller is saying? Show that you are listening by giving little grunts (verbal nods) and by asking questions to clarify, if necessary. Do you wait for the main purpose of the call to be explained, or do you jump in with what you *think* is the right response? Listen until the caller comes to a natural pause.

Transferring calls

If you have to transfer a call to someone else, there are things you can do to make it easier for the caller and the new receiver:
- transfer to the right person or department. If you do not know who this is
  - tell the caller you will call him/her back and take the caller's name and number. Explain to the caller what you are going to do
  - find out who is the right person to deal with the matter
  - get that person to ring the caller back, or do so yourself
- tell the new receiver who is calling and a little bit about what (s)he wants; this saves the caller having to start from scratch. Do not just ring another number and transfer the caller without contacting the new receiver yourself first
- tell the caller the name and position or section of the new receiver
- transfer the call and let the caller know you are doing so

Misunderstandings

How do you overcome the problems of a poor caller without appearing impatient, rude or dumb? (The caller thinks, 'Well, you ought to understand'.) Do not ask the caller to repeat what s(he) has said. Instead, say back to the caller what you think was said – the caller will soon correct you if you are wrong.

Irate callers

How do you deal with an irate caller? Get impatient and shout back? Let the caller run out of steam, listen calmly and be polite. Do not take it personally; the caller is usually getting at the company, not at you. Try to make the caller understand that you will do all you can to help sort the matter out. If a mistake has been made, apologise, get the caller's mind off what went wrong and try to get the caller to say what s(he) wants done now. The same approach would be just as effective for irate callers to your telephone at home.

Saying no

How do you say 'No' when you have to? Say 'No, no way'? Instead, say something like 'I'm sorry, I/we can't do so and so; *however* I/we might be able to .....'. Try to offer an acceptable alternative, and use the word 'however'. 'However' is more positive than 'but', which could sound rather reluctant or grudging to your caller.

Hanging on

What do you do when you have to find someone or something? Say 'Hang on a minute'? Let the caller know what you are doing; putting on 'hold' or loudspeaker. If you speak with your hand over the mouthpiece, or leave the handset on the desk, the caller can hear what you are saying. Say you are going to put the caller on 'hold' for a moment, and press the mute button.

Telephone practice

- Listen to other people making a call or answering the telephone. Make a mental note of the things they do well or badly.
- Next time you make a call or answer the telephone, analyse what you did well or badly:
  - how did you identify yourself?
  - what did you forget?
  - how much time did you waste?
  - were you speaking to the right person?
  - did you check names, addresses, figures etc?

  Be strict with yourself and decide what you could do better next time.
- Look at the layout round the telephone you usually use. Answer 'yes' or 'no' to each of these questions:
  - is the telephone on the correct side for you?
  - are the pen/pencil and notepad handy?
  - have you got enough space for writing messages?
  - have you got handy the telephone numbers you frequently use?
  - can you use all the necessary facilities on your machine?

  If you answered 'no' to any of those questions, do you need to do anything about it? If so, what are you going to do?

Answering machines

Talking to machines

Some people do not like talking to answering machines – why? Probably one of the reasons is the lack of feedback. It feels very strange talking to something which gives you no response – even the most unhelpful receiver occasionally gives a grunt!

What is the best way to talk to an answering machine? Probably this is another case for KISS (Keep It Short and Simple); think about what would be the most appropriate for the receiver.

What can be very helpful to the receiver is to know the date *and* the time you made your call. This can be particularly valuable if calls are picked up remotely by the receiver, who may be away from the answering machine for some time. You may feel it appropriate just to leave your name and number and the time of your call. Do always leave your number, even if you are a regular caller. It could be that if the receiver is picking up your call remotely, your number is not readily to hand, and you might have to wait for a response – which could be inconvenient for you both.

If, as a caller, you have to leave a definite message, it could be helpful to jot down the details and use the notes as a 'crib sheet' to dictate the information onto the answering machine. Some people ring off and start again so that they are prepared for the machine. Remember the importance of clarity of speech and information – the machine cannot (yet!) ask you to repeat something which is not quite clear.

One of the difficulties callers often have in leaving a message on an answering machine is how to finish. Listen to some messages if you can – they are sometimes very funny, without intending to be of course. You can feel very silly saying goodbye to nothing. However, all that is needed is a simple statement like 'Thank you, goodbye' or 'I look forward to hearing from you', and perhaps a repeat of the call-back number.

Machine owners

As the owner of an answering machine, you can help to make the caller feel comfortable when speaking to it by the recorded message you leave. This covers not only the content but the way in which it is presented. What are the essentials for a recorded greeting? Basically, something which should re-assure the caller that the right number has been obtained, and that a message would be welcomed.

It is a good idea not to make your recorded message too long. This is particularly relevant when a caller is trying to contact you from a public telephone, especially one with a coinbox. It can be very frustrating to have your coin run out before the answering machine has even finished its greeting, let alone given you the chance to leave your message.

Try to make your recorded message as friendly and as welcoming to the caller as though you were answering the call in person; either as yourself, or as the representative of your organisation. The caller might be feeling frustrated that you are not there, so a caller-friendly response is even more important. Practise different types of message on a cassette recorder before you finally decide which format to use – or, having recorded a message, ring yourself up to hear how it sounds. 'Fun' messages can be acceptable on private lines, but are inappropriate for business use.

Your answering machine is just as much a part of your business image as your company stationery. If you were listening to the message on your machine, what impression would you get?

On the telephone – checklist

CALLER

DO	DON'T
• be clear about objective of call	• plunge straight into detail
• think clearly before dialling	• make asides
• arrange material logically	• interrupt
• express information clearly	• speak: too quickly
• use understandable language	too slowly
• give details concisely	with your mouth
• smile down the telephone	full
• keep it short and simple (KISS)	• shout
• be sincere	• whisper
• consider the receiver	• mumble
	• answer back
	• be: rude
	funny
	flippant
	insincere
	• use jargon

RECEIVER

DO
- give a greeting and then say who you are
- listen until the caller has told you the whole story
- have a pad and pencil handy
- have somewhere specific to put written messages
- keep the caller informed about what is going on

DON'T
- leave people hanging on
- talk with your hand over the mouthpiece
- talk to someone else as you pick up the handset
- forget to pass on messages
- transfer people without warning (see checklist below)

TRANSFERRING CALLS

DO
- find the right person
- speak to that person yourself
- tell the new receiver the caller's name and subject of call
- tell the caller the new receiver's name and position

DON'T
- say it's nothing to do with you.
- transfer without checking the new receiver is there
- forget to ring back or get the new receiver to ring back if necessary

ANSWERING MACHINE

CALLER DO
- give name, number, day and time of call
- repeat numbers
- make sure your message is clear and definite
- sign off positively, rather than fading out

OWNER DO
- make sure your recorded message is short and caller-friendly
- ring yourself up and see how you sound
- suggest caller leaves day and time of message

> **KISS**

6 Talking to Customers or Clients

In this chapter:
- Who are customers or clients?
- Your image – first impressions
- Your body language
- Questioning
- Listening
- Language
- Tone of voice
- Last impressions

 ## Who are customers or clients?

Customers or clients are anyone who comes to you because they need what you have to offer. You are the professional, with the knowledge, the skills, the merchandise or the advice. Sometimes they are called customers (in shops, restaurants and banks, for example), sometimes they are called clients (by lawyers, hairdressers and counsellors, for example), sometimes they are called patients (by doctors, dentists and nurses, for example), and sometimes they are just thought of as the general public (by civil servants or the police, for example).

So a customer is *anyone* who has a need. This includes your own colleagues or workmates, who come to you for advice, forms, statistics, typing, computer programs or knowledge. If you are a teacher or a lecturer, your customers are your pupils or students.

The important part is that you are the one with the knowledge, skill, merchandise or whatever it is, and the way you present yourself to your customers, clients, patients etc is all part of the process of meeting your customers' needs.

Throughout this chapter you will be asked to think about the various aspects of talking to customers or clients. Base what you do on your own job, or, if you are still at school or college, base your thoughts either on a job you know about personally (a Saturday or holiday job, perhaps) or one which you know as a customer. A hairdresser is quite a good one; there are very few people who do not go to a hairdresser from time to time.

Practice 1 – Who are your customers/clients/patients etc?

1 Choose the job you are going to use as a basis.
2 Make a list of all the people, or types of people, who come to you for your professional advice, service etc.
3 If you are at school or college, or are very new to a job, think of one of which you have personal knowledge.
4 If you work behind the scenes in an office, warehouse, canteen, factory, etc, make a list of the colleagues or workmates who come to you or rely on you for your skills, advice, help, etc.

There are very few people who have no customers at all.

Your image – first impressions

People come to you as a professional – hairdresser, secretary, surgeon, banker, porter, actor, chiropodist, decorator. What do they expect to see? They expect to see someone who fits their idea of what you should be like.

Many people wear uniforms, which helps their customers and helps them as well. Even if your job does not require you to wear a white coat, an overall or a special kind of hat, you still wear a sort of uniform to work, (a suit, skirt and blouse or a track suit perhaps).

Your own clothes help you to create the image of what other people want and expect to see.

The same applies to your personal belongings and your surroundings. A business person carries a briefcase, not a plastic bag; a football referee wears a whistle, not a gold chain. A doctor's reception area must look clean and clinical, although restful; a fashion boutique has to look bright and alive.

First impressions are very powerful. What your customers or clients see in the first moments of meeting you will probably colour the whole of their dealings with you.

How highly do you rate? Is your personal appearance what your customers want and expect to see? Whatever sort of uniform you wear – clothes provided or personal clothes – is it clean, neat, attractive, suitable for its purpose? How about your personal belongings and your surroundings? Do they match the total image of you, and what your clients are looking for?

Practice 2 – How attractive are you?

Imagine you are a customer or client or whatever coming to see you. If you are using the hairdresser example, imagine you are a customer going into the shop.

1 Mark yourself out of 10 for personal appearance.

2 Stand or sit where a client or customer would stand or sit, and jot down:
• the parts which match the image you want to project
• the parts which do not match that image

3 Write down what alterations you are going to make to improve the total image.

Your body language

Your body language plays an important part in getting a conversation or a transaction off to a good start. Put yourself in the other person's shoes, and decide what they would like to see you doing as they approach you.

What they do *not* want to see is you:
- talking to a colleague or workmate
- leaning on something, looking bored
- with your head buried in books or papers
- looking rushed and harassed, as if you have no time for them
- with your eyes glued to your VDU
- with your arms folded, looking closed

What they *do* want to see is you:
- looking directly at them
- looking friendly and welcoming
- standing or sitting upright, looking confident
- smiling in greeting, if that is appropriate
- with your arms and hands looking friendly and welcoming

If you start off looking as other people want you to look, you start off on the right foot, and your body language is less likely to get out of control once you are deep in conversation.

Practice 3 – Be aware of your body language

Next time you see someone coming towards you wanting something, whether you are sitting or standing, be aware of your body language. If you are using the hairdressing example, make a note of what you actually see.

1 Make a mental note of what you are doing with your arms, legs, feet and general posture.
   Is that what you normally do?

2 Notice whether you are smiling in greeting.
   Is that what you normally do?

3 If there is some aspect of your body language which could be improved, make a mental note of what it is, and try out the improvement on the next person who comes to you. See if it makes any difference in your feelings towards them, or in their attitude to you. Try this out particularly on someone you do not like or someone you perhaps fear.

Questioning

People who come to you for something sometimes know exactly what they want, but more often than not you have to question them so that you can clarify for them and for yourself exactly what their needs are. Even if someone senior to you asks or tells you to do something, it is often useful to check, by asking questions, exactly what is required so that you get it right. For example if someone says to you

"Could you do that for me by Wednesday, please?",

it is worthwhile saying

"What time on Wednesday?"

If the answer comes back

"Oh, I need it for 9.00 o'clock"

you know you have got to get it done by the end of Tuesday afternoon or evening.

Questioning is a natural part of identifying exactly what someone wants – identifying your customers' needs. If you are a skilled questioner you are much more likely to identify those needs accurately and get it right first time, which pleases the customer and saves you a whole lot of hassle.

You have probably heard of open and closed questions. If you have, do you use them properly yourself? If you have not, this is what they are and how they should be used.

Closed questions

These are questions which can be answered 'yes' or 'no' without adding anything further. For example, if you say:

"Do you like cake?"

the answer can be 'yes' or 'no', and that is the end of the conversation. Of course people often add a sentence or phrase, such as 'Yes, but not fruit cake' or 'No, it's usually too rich', which adds something to your knowledge of what they do or do not like, but they do not have to do this.

So closed questions usually get very limited or limiting answers. They can be very useful in certain circumstances, when you want to limit someone's choice, or persuade them to come to a decision. For example:

"Would you prefer 10.00 or 10.30?"

is more limiting than saying

"When would you like to come in?"

which is an open question.

Open questions

These are questions which begin with 'what', 'why', 'where', 'when', 'how' and 'who'. They are questions which cannot possibly be answered by just 'yes' or 'no', so they give the questioner much more information.

If you keep on asking this sort of question, you can learn a lot about your customers' requirements and can meet their needs more effectively. For example, consider this conversation between a hairdresser and a client; as you read it, decide which are the open questions and which are closed.

The client is new to the establishment and has come in for a cut and blow dry, and the hairdresser needs to find out exactly what the customer needs.
"How do you like it cut?"
"Oh, fairly short on top, but a bit longer at the back."
"How about over the ears?"
"Just a bit shorter than it is now."
"Do you like it tapered towards the back of the neck?"
"No."
"What style would you prefer?"
"More rounded, I think."

And at the blow-drying stage:
"Do you have styling mousse?"
"Yes, please."
"How often do you normally have to wash your hair?"
"About every three days."
"Is that too hot?"
"No, that's fine."

"Who normally does your hair for you?"
"My hairdresser at home – I'm only visiting."

So the hairdresser has found out not only how the client wants his or her hair cut and dried on this occasion, (s)he has also found out that the person takes good care of his or her hair (reasonably frequent washing) and that he or she is not likely to become a permanent client (only visiting).

As a customer yourself, you expect to be asked questions by your doctor, dentist, sales assistant, teacher, travel agent, waitress, insurance broker and so on. In the same way your customers, wherever they are, will expect you to ask questions of them. The skill lies in asking the right questions.

Practice 4 – Ask the right questions

1 Listen to someone you work with dealing with their customers. See if you can decide whether they are using open or closed questions, and whether they get all the information they need in as short a time as possible.
2 Write down some open and closed questions which you use when dealing with your own customers, clients, etc. If you are using the hairdressing example, choose a different part of the process, like doing highlights or perming.
3 Next time you are trying to clarify exactly what someone wants, analyse the sort of questions you are using. This works just as well when you are trying to get things straight with your lecturers, teachers or trainers.

Listening

If you ask questions you have to listen to the answers, and you need to listen to all sorts of things your customers say. Listen with your brain, as well as with your ears.

Listen to:
- the story: the facts
- the person: their personality and circumstances

- the underlying message: often what is not said is every bit as important as what is said

You need to concentrate, without interrupting, and not jump to conclusions before you have heard the whole story. It is amazing how often people interrupt, particularly people who are themselves rather talkative.

Some people are very difficult to listen to, because they cannot get the words out very easily, or you cannot understand what they are saying, or they go rambling on without saying anything very pertinent or interesting. You have to be patient and keep asking questions until you get the whole story – facts, circumstances and underlying message.

Read this conversation between a car salesman and his customer. From the answers the customer gives, see if you can sort out the facts, something about the customer's circumstances and any underlying message (what is not said). The questions at the end should help you. Unfortunately you have only the words to read, and cannot hear the tone of voice used.

"What kind of car had you in mind?"
"I want a small car for driving round town. Two-door, I think, economical on petrol and easy to park."
"Automatic?"
"Oh, no. I'm quite happy with ordinary gears."
"This basic model comes with radio and power-assisted steering. It's got good ventilation and heating and plenty of leg room, even though it's small. If you want central locking, electrically-operated windows and tinted glass you'll have to look at the next model in the range."
"I only need the very basics for this car. We can always use the other one if we need more space. I suppose it runs on unleaded petrol?"
"Oh yes, all the new models do now."

What did the salesman learn about his customer? Answer these questions:
a) What sort of car does the customer want? (The facts)
b) How knowledgeable is the customer about cars? (The person)
c) What sort of lifestyle does the customer lead? (The circumstances)
d) Which political party might the customer vote for? (The underlying message)
e) Was the customer a man or a woman? (The salesman would obviously know this!)

Your answers are probably based on your own experience and pre-conceived ideas, but you could be wrong! For example, did you think the customer was knowledgeable about cars, just because he or she was obviously experienced in driving? Did you assume that the second car was a family car, and that 'we' were husband and wife? The 'we' could be business partners. Did you decide that the buyer is a man or a woman without really thinking it through? The answer here is that you really cannot tell. Beware of jumping to conclusions based on your prejudices or pre-conceived ideas!

People reveal a great deal about themselves if you listen to them intelligently and give them your full attention. How good a listener are you?

Practice 5 – Listen

1 Listen to two people talking to each other – at work, at home, school or college, or travelling. Decide how well they listen, how often they interrupt, how much they concentrate and whether they come to any decisions, or are just chatting.
2 When you want something, analyse how well other people listen to you. Do they jump to conclusions, interrupt, get the full picture, or what?
3 The next time someone comes to you for something, analyse your own listening technique:
   - what are the facts?
   - what did you learn about the person?
   - was there any underlying message?
   - did you concentrate?
   - did you interrupt?
   - did you jump to conclusions?

4 Decide what you could do better next time.

Language

Other chapters in this book (Chapters 2 and 11 in particular) deal with the importance of speaking clearly. Here we are thinking about the *words* you use because people are coming to you as clients, customers, patients or the general public.

Earlier you were considering your body language at the start of a conversation. Think now about what you actually say when someone comes to you as a customer. Are you the sort of person who just says 'Yes?', or 'Well?', or even 'Come!' when someone knocks on your door? Those are very abrupt greetings and hardly likely to inspire your customers with confidence. 'Good morning', 'Good afternoon', or 'Hello' are much more friendly. So is 'Hi', but some people find that too familiar.

You have to adapt your language to your customer or client. 'Sir' and 'Madam' are right in some circumstances. 'Dear' and 'Luv' can sometimes be acceptable, but many people get very offended if people use those sorts of words, so you have to be careful. If at all possible, use the customer's name; it sounds more friendly and cannot give offence – unless you use the first name when the customer would prefer to be called Mr, Mrs, Miss or Ms. Think about each individual and adapt your language accordingly. Do not say 'Cheers' when it should be 'Thank you', nor 'Sure' when 'OK' or even 'Yes' would be better.

Consider, as well, the technical terms you use. Every trade and profession has its own vocabulary which outsiders do not necessarily know – the professional jargon. It is thoughtless to use words which you know people will not understand, and very rude to talk to a colleague or workmate using jargon in front of a third person, as if they were not there. As usual, put yourself in your customer's shoes and use the language he or she can relate to.

What do you do with people who cannot understand you? Perhaps they come from a different part of the country, or a different part of the world. Perhaps they are deaf. Try doing this:
- stand or sit looking directly at them
- don't shout
- speak slowly and distinctly, separating the words
- smile
- use gestures to demonstrate
- watch their eyes for understanding
- use simple language, not slang or jargon
- say things in a different way, if necessary
- have patience

With patience and understanding, human beings usually manage to communicate successfully – particularly if someone wants something from you anyway.

Practice 6 – Language

1 Write down a list of words which are technical terms or jargon in your own work. If you are at school or college, choose a subject or hobby you know well, and use that as a base.
2 Take each word in turn, and say aloud (on your own if you prefer) the alternative words you would use when talking to someone who knows nothing about your area or subject. If you cannot think of another word, try to describe, out loud, what you mean. For example, if someone does not understand what you mean by VDU, you could say 'the screen'.
3 If you have a cassette recorder, use that to hear how clearly you speak.

Tone of voice

As we saw in Chapter 1, the words which you use convey very little of the message to someone else. Your body language conveys a lot more, and so does the tone of your voice.

It is not difficult to understand what people mean when they use their voice in certain ways. You can soon tell when someone is angry, tearful, bored or excited, even if you cannot hear or understand the words. But it is quite difficult to control your own tone of voice so that it conveys what you want it to convey, and not, sometimes, what you really feel.

Use your cassette recorder again, and listen to yourself saying the same phrase in all sorts of different ways. Say 'COULD YOU JUST EXPLAIN THIS TO ME' as if you were:
- angry
- bored
- interested
- excited
- depressed
- concerned
- in a hurry

If you have no cassette recorder, say the phrase aloud in those different ways anyway.

The problem is that we sometimes, without meaning to, use the wrong tone of voice and convey something quite different from what we intended. It is very easy to sound bored if you are really not interested in what someone is saying. If you are interested, then there is no problem, but if you are not, you have to put on a little bit of an act if you are going to deal properly with your customer. Your body language and tone of voice will give you away, if you are not very careful.

For example, supposing the hairdresser finds that the customer has got split ends, and wants to advise on how to do something about it. If the hairdresser is not careful about the tone of voice – if he or she sounds disgusted or critical – the customer will feel really offended or put down and sit there in misery. The hairdresser must sound concerned, neutral and matter-of-fact, so that the good advice can be taken and acted upon.

Practice 7 – Listen to the tone

1 Listen to the tone of voice your colleagues or workmates use with their customers, clients and so on. Decide whose tone comes across best.
2 If you think your own voice sounds uninterested or harsh or arrogant or whining, or anything which it should not be when you are speaking to your customers, try to identify what is wrong with it, and put it right. One of the most common faults is people sounding too busy to bother with you.

Last impressions

What impression does your customer or client or patient or colleague or friend walk away with in the end? It will depend on all the things you have been considering in this chapter and also on the way in which you end the conversation. Do you remember to say 'Thank you', 'Goodbye', 'Hope it goes well' and all the other courtesies you know you should use? It is a little thing, but it does make a difference, and makes your customers want to have dealings with you again.

68

How well do you present yourself when talking to customers or clients – from first to last?

	Points to remember from this chapter

- A customer is anyone who wants something from you
  – you are the professional, and should be in control
- What are your customers' first impressions of you and your surroundings?
- Are you using the right body language?
  – open, confident, welcoming etc
- Do you find out all you need to know?
  – are you asking the right sort of questions?
- How good a listener are you?
  – do you pick up all the details you need?
  – do you interrupt, or jump to conclusions?
- What is your language like?
  – do you use too much jargon?
- Does the tone of your voice put people off, or do they like talking to you?
- What is other people's lasting impression of you as a professional?

7 Asking the Boss for Something

In this chapter:
- Who is 'the boss'?
- Assertive, not aggressive
- Simple requests
- More complicated requirements
- Knowing the boss
- Timing
- Presenting your case
- The outcome

Who is 'the boss'?

'The boss', in this chapter, is the person who makes the decisions, who can say 'yes' or 'no' to your request. It could be your teacher, your lecturer, your supervisor, your manager. The final decision-maker could be someone a bit remote from you, whom you have to approach through your teacher, lecturer, supervisor or manager. It is important to recognise who exactly is the decision-maker, and work towards that person, even if you have to work through someone else.

To help you decide who is the decision-maker, you need to be quite clear in your own mind exactly what it is you want to ask. It could be anything from some unscheduled time off to a new computer system. Whatever it is, the steps to take to get a successful outcome (ie get what you want) are the same.

Assertive, not aggressive

Some people think you have to be aggressive to get what you want, but this is not true. You may have to be assertive, which is something quite different. Being assertive is about knowing what you want and going the right way about getting it. It is about not being content with second-best. It is about approaching people in the right way, at the right time and having the courage to put forward your point of view in an adult, logical way. It is *not* about storming in to see the boss and demanding in a loud voice that something shall be done – that is aggression. If you are aggressive, you are much less likely to succeed in getting what you want.

Being assertive is about preparing the ground, working with and through people, not against them. It is about timing, presenting your case in the best possible light and using a positive approach. It is about getting what you want (providing it is something reasonable) without upsetting the system or the people – making the system and the people work for you. Sometimes it is necessary to try to change the system and the attitude of the people. It is often quite possible to do this in a gentle and subtle way; this is the approach you will probably have to take if you are working from the bottom upwards, rather than from the top down.

It is amazing what you can achieve by persistence, logic, persuasion and negotiation, rather than by force and aggression. Sometimes it can seem as if you are not getting anywhere, but when you look back, you realise that you have moved forward quite a lot, without appearing pushy or insensitive. Sometimes you will not achieve the goal you have set yourself, and find that you have had to compromise, but that is all part of the skill of negotiation and knowing when to accept 'no' for an answer, and to accept it graciously.

For example, suppose two of you are eating out and find yourselves sitting near the kitchen when you would prefer to be near the window. There is an empty table nearer the window for four, but all the window tables are full. What do you do?

a) stay where you are, although it is rather uncomfortable
b) move to the empty table without asking
c) ask to move to the empty table
d) demand a table by the window

If you choose a) you are accepting second-best, because the best in this instance is the table nearer the window for four.

If you choose b) you will probably antagonise the restaurant staff and, unless you are very thick-skinned, will eat your meal in an unpleasant atmosphere which will make it less enjoyable. You will have been aggressive.

If you choose c) you could be upsetting the system and the people. But if you ask politely if you can move, and put forward a good reason for doing so (eg because you need space to look at some papers, or you would prefer to be nearer the non-smoking area), the people – ie the maître d'hotel or the waiter/waitress – are much more likely to move you happily. Give a positive reason for moving (something which will help you) rather than a negative reason (it is too uncomfortable nearer the kitchen); the first is meeting your needs, the second is criticising the restaurant. If you move to the table nearer the window and enjoy your meal, you will have been assertive, not aggressive, and will have achieved most of what you want.

If you choose d) you are probably being aggressive and are asking the impossible anyway. If you are desperate to sit by the window, offer an alternative – for example, suggest you will wait until a table is free. Again you will have achieved your goal, but will have shown you are prepared to put yourself out to do so.

Not all situations are as cut-and-dried as this, but in most circumstances there is room for negotiation, alternatives and improvement. One of the secrets of success is knowing what you want and preparing the ground to achieve your goal.

Preparation

If you rush into asking the boss for something without doing a bit (or in some cases a lot) of preparation, you are less likely to achieve your objective. Consider two situations: asking for time off and asking for a new photocopier. Preparation for the first will be far less complicated than it will for the second, but still needs to be done.

Simple requests

What preparation do you need to do to ask for something fairly simple, like an unscheduled day off? This is the situation:

- You are going away for the weekend and would get back on Sunday night, but it would be much better if you could have Monday away as well and come in on Tuesday morning

Your preparation should be:
a) Know exactly what you want
b) Judge whether it is a possibility or not
c) Prepare to counter objections
d) Decide where you are willing to compromise if necessary.

a) Know exactly what you want
In this case it is simple – you want Monday off.

b) Judge whether it is a possibility or not
If you know that at work you have some holiday due to you or, at school or college it is just possible to wangle a day away at that time of the year, the day off is possible.

Have you any deadlines to meet, meetings to attend or are you desperately needed because of staff shortages? If the answer is 'no', again the day off is a possibility. If the answer is 'yes' to any of these, forget it.

It will be easier to get what you want if your work is normally good and completed on time.

c) Prepare to counter objections
Put yourself in your boss's shoes and think what objections might be raised. For example, you will miss a particular lesson or lecture, or you are down to do a certain job.

Prepare your counter-suggestion: for example, one of your friends will take notes for you, or someone has agreed to help out at that particular job, or someone else is expected back at work.

Make it *easy* for your boss to say 'Yes'.

d) Decide where you are willing to compromise if necessary
Would you be able to work a little extra time on the Friday, or give in some work a day sooner? Would you be able to return at mid-day on the Monday, so you only miss half a day?

If you have some alternatives up your sleeve and, if necessary, put them forward as positive and helpful suggestions, you will often find your boss will agree to everything you have asked for anyway. It shows that you have been thinking responsibly and are prepared to give a little extra to get what you want. Half a loaf is better than none at all.

More complicated requirements

If what you want is more complicated, like asking for a new
photocopier, you can still follow the same steps, but in greater depth
and more detail:
a) Know exactly what you want
b) Judge whether it is a possibility or not
c) Prepare to counter objections
d) Decide where you are willing to compromise if necessary.

a) Know exactly what you want
It is not enough to say that you need a new photocopier without
being able to state why you want it and what you want.

If you need a new copier because yours is always breaking down
through over use or age, you need to prepare firm statistics over a
given period, say a week or two, of:
• how often the machine is not working
• the cost of maintenance, if this is relevant
• how much time you and others have wasted because you have had
  to go elsewhere for photocopies
• any deadlines which have been missed as a result of no
  photocopier etc

If you collect figures in terms of time converted into money, so much
the better.

If you need a new copier because there are too few copiers for
too many people, or because the copiers are too far away, you need
to collect evidence of time spent queuing for the copier, time spent
walking round the building etc.

If you can prove satisfactorily that you really do need a new
copier, you should also prepare the ground for suggesting what you
do want. Do you need another machine of the same size, a machine
with greater capacity which is quicker, extra add-on facilities like an
automatic sheet feeder, or a collator, or what? Decide which is the
best possible solution, collect details and cost it all out. Show how
cost-effective a new copier would be, how savings could be made
and therefore what benefit it would be to the company.

Obviously this amount of preparation takes time, but if it results
in better working conditions for you and others, it is time well
invested.

b) Judge whether it is possibility or not
Only circumstances in your school, college or place of work will tell
you whether you are asking the impossible. If the whole office has

recently been refurbished, with all new equipment and furniture, or if you know for sure there is just no money available, forget it – for the moment. There is no point in wasting time and energy seeking the impossible, although what at first seems an impossibility can sometimes turn out to be quite workable.

c) Prepare to counter objections
If you have done your homework carefully and prepared a good case for your photocopier, there should not be too many objections. This is where your careful preparation will pay off.

However, some people seem to like to raise objections on principle, so you must be prepared to answer likely objections – lack of time, lack of money, present photocopier not properly used, and so on. Put yourself in your boss's shoes and try to anticipate what objections she or he may raise. This is particularly important if your boss is not the decision-maker; you need your boss with you, not against you, and s(he) needs all the ammunition you can gather to go and fight the photocopier battle on your behalf. Setting out the benefits to the company is a very powerful weapon, but only if they are true benefits based on facts.

d) Decide where you are willing to compromise if necessary
If a totally new copier is shown to be out of the question, have at the back of your mind some acceptable compromise, like better access to another machine, tighter control of the use of the machine, less expensive facilities, a secondhand machine etc. Do not show your hand too soon, but if necessary show that you understand the position and are prepared to go some way to accepting a compromise, and to putting yourself out to do so. Half a loaf is better than no bread.

Practice 1 – Do your preparation

1 Identify a situation where you know you have got to ask someone for something, even if it is only a very small favour. Try to choose something which you can actually try out later.
2 Prepare your ground by writing down:
   a) exactly what it is you want
   b) whether it is a possibility, and what makes it possible or impossible
   c) what objections might be raised, and how you can counteract these

d) what alternatives there are which you are prepared to accept.

3 Keep these notes by you, and add to them when you come to the next Practice section.

Knowing the boss

If someone asks you for something, what is your first instinct? Do you automatically say 'yes', and then perhaps find that you cannot oblige? Do you automatically say 'no' and then start thinking of ways in which you can help? Is your instinct to say 'I'll think about it' or perhaps 'I'll see what I can do'?

You need to know a little about how your own boss's mind works so that you can ask for what you want in the best possible way.

Here is a table of some of the ways in which people think and work, and your possible strategy for making those characteristics work for you.

IF YOUR BOSS	TRY
• is the sort of person who likes a lot of detail	• to present your case in as much detail as possible, thinking of all the angles and objections
• likes time to consider things	• not to ask for snap decisions; give the person time to think it through
• can make snap decisions	• to put forward (verbally or in writing) the main points of the case you want to make. Give your boss a KISS and 'Keep it Short and Simple'
• automatically says 'no'	• to give her or him time to come round. Be persistent and do not take the first 'no' for an answer – it might be a ploy to

	see how sincere or serious you are!
• automatically says 'yes', and then regrets it	• not to give her or him cause to regret the decision
• is approachable	• not to become over-familiar or take advantage
• is not approachable	• to prepare a watertight case and pick the best moment to ask for what you want
• is not the decision-maker	• to get her or him on your side
• is indecisive	• to pin her or him down. Keep asking questions until you get a final 'yes' or 'no'

If your boss's characteristics are not described here, try to identify what those characteristics are, and how you could use them to your advantage.

Practice 2 – What is your boss like?

1 Keep in mind what it is you are going to ask (Practice 1) and write down how your boss is likely to react to your request – use the list above to help you.
2 Write down, in detail, what you need to do to use those characteristics to your advantage. For example, if your boss is a person who makes snap decisions, as soon as that decision is made you should act quickly to get things going – book the holiday, ask the photocopier rep to call etc.

Keep in mind what you want, and be as specific as you can about what you have to do.

Timing

There is a great skill in choosing the right time to ask for something, particularly if you are dealing with very busy people who are themselves not necessarily good managers of their own time. Sometimes you literally have to catch them in the corridor, but this is not usually a very satisfactory way of getting them to make decisions in your favour.

There are bad times to ask for something; these are normally:

- as people arrive, before they have had time to take their coat off or sit down.
- when they are frantically busy with other people and telephone calls
- when they are really concentrating on something with someone else
- when they are flying off to a meeting, or lunch, or at the end of the day
- when a disaster has occurred or is happening
- when they are in a bad mood

You might wonder whether there is ever a good time to ask for something, but even very busy people have the odd free moment now and again, and most people will make time for their students or staff.

Check whether it is a good time of day by asking your boss whether she or he has a few moments to spare. Have your request and arguments ready in case that time is then and there. If the requirement is a more complicated matter (like the photocopier) it is usually best to book the time in the diary, and to give your boss the necessary papers to read beforehand. If you do make an appointment, be sure to stick to it.

Practice 3 – When is the best time to approach your boss?

Consider what it is you are going to ask, the preparations you have made and the characteristics of your boss. Add what you think is the best time to approach her or him, and whether you think you should book some time in the diary or whether an informal few minutes will do.

 ## Presenting your case

There are three main things to consider when you get as far as asking for what you want:
- your image, which includes your body language
- what you want to say
- how you are going to say it

Your image, which includes your body language

It is not normally necessary to do anything different about your dress or general appearance, because you are communicating in the normal course of your studies or work. It is not like a formal interview or an exam. Your body language is important, though.

If it is the custom to knock on the door, do so. If you do not normally sit down with your boss, wait until you are asked to do so. Ask for what you want in a confident, direct sort of way, as though you expect the answer to be 'yes'. Stand or sit looking confident and relaxed, not nervous or aggressive. Look your boss straight in the eye, wait until you have her or his full attention, keep your hands and feet still and look as though you are going to make a reasonable request – which you are.

If you get this sort of detail right, you will probably get off to a good start.

What you want to say

This is where your preparation comes in. Say exactly what you want, and back it up with the points you have prepared. Have a practice beforehand if necessary, so that when the time comes you do not stumble and say a lot of 'ums' and 'ers'.

If you have written down the points to make, go through them in sequence, giving your boss time to read and understand each point. Make sure you have a copy each.

Answer any questions clearly and directly. If you do not know the answer, say so and offer to find out.

Make sure that you both understand what is agreed between you, and what you are both going to do next. Repeat the points which have been agreed, saying something like:

"So you want me to ...... and you'll ......" or
"So that's OK if I ......"

How you are going to say it

The tone of your voice is important. Try not to sound anxious or pleading. Make your voice neutral and speak slowly at first; people often gabble if they are nervous.

Listen and do not interrupt if your boss is trying to clarify points. If you interrupt you will not understand the questions you have to answer.

Make sure that everything you present in writing matches what you want to say. A scruffy piece of paper, illegibly handwritten, will not improve your case for a new photocopier; a beautifully typed request for a day off is not normally necessary.

Keep calm, even if you seem to be losing the battle. When people get angry, logic goes out of the window. If you can stay calm and think straight, you will be able to put forward a different point or suggest one of those compromises you have got up your sleeve.

The outcome

There are three possibilities:
- you get exactly what you want
- you get a provisional 'yes'
- you get a definite 'no'

If you get exactly what you want, fine – go ahead and do whatever was agreed.

If you get a provisional 'yes', or even a reluctant 'no', offer to do something further (get more facts, change the time etc) so that a firm decision can be reached in the long run.

If you get a definite 'no', accept it gracefully. If you did all your preparation and presented your case well, there is nothing further you can do – for the moment. Circumstances change, and you might be able to ask the same sort of thing again in a short time or at some time in the future.

80

Whatever the outcome, thank your boss – either for saying 'yes' or for listening to your request. You are paving the way for the future, and might need to ask another favour another time.

And finally, if the favour was granted, when you have done or got whatever it was (after the weekend or when the new photocopier arrives), remember to say thank you again. It will make your boss feel good, and it will make you feel good, too.

Practice 4 – Ask for what you want and analyse what happened

1 Having made all your preparations, go to the boss (or whoever it is) and ask for what you want.

2 Afterwards analyse what went on. Answer these questions:
   - did I get what I wanted?
   - what did I do right?
   - what did I do wrong?
   - what could I do better, or differently next time?
   - what will my boss think of me now?
   - how well did I present myself and my case?

Points to remember from this chapter

- Be assertive, not aggressive
- Prepare what you want to ask:
  - know exactly what you want
  - is it possible?
  - what are the likely objections?
  - can you compromise?
- Study your boss and judge how and when to approach
- Present yourself and your case well
- Accept victory or defeat graciously
- Analyse your self presentation skills
- Decide how you can improve

8 Showing Someone How to do Something

In this chapter:
- Formal instruction
- Job breakdown, preparation and use
- Giving instruction: prepare
  - instruct
  - put to work
  - check

Formal instruction

In the normal course of a working day you could be involved in showing people how to do things. This could range from simple things which could be done in passing, like straightening up a display ticket, where to write a figure on a form or which disk to use on the computer for a particular program.

There will also be occasions when you will have to give instruction on practical subjects in a more complete and formal way. This chapter is concerned with an approach to this form of training activity. Instruction should be given in a methodical way, ensuring that nothing is overlooked, while taking into account the existing knowledge of the learner.

You need to be confident about *what* you are going to teach and how you are going to teach it. The way you set about showing someone how to do something will have considerable effect on how well the learner learns the task and can perform it competently. Your own presentation skills have a large part to play in this.

This chapter covers making your own notes to use when giving instruction (job breakdown) and advice on how to use these notes to make sure the learner learns.

 ## Job breakdown

One of the reasons why learners do not learn something quickly and thoroughly is that the instructor does not teach the learner the whole job, or teaches it in the wrong order. Few people can learn large chunks of anything all at once, so:
- practical instruction should be given
  - in stages
  - in a logical sequence
- the job content needs to be broken down into its component parts

Job breakdown is a way of doing this. The instructor writes down, in note form, the stages and the key points the learner must learn, and uses these notes when giving instruction.

Preparation

There are three things to do when making a job breakdown:
- *do the job* thoroughly yourself to make sure that it is right
- *select the stages* (*what* has to be done) by doing the job through again. When you come to a natural break in the sequence, this will probably be a suitable portion for the learner to master
- *find the key points* (*how* things are to be done) by going through the job again, stage by stage, and writing down the key points within each stage. These are points which might: affect quality; ensure safety; make the work easier; ensure hygiene standards; give special information and so on

COMMON FAULTS IN MAKING JOB BREAKDOWNS
- Starting to write the job breakdown without doing the job
- Writing long sentences for a stage, instead of a simple statement
- Handwriting difficult to read (use block capitals)
- Writing words in a stage different from those which will be used when giving instruction (talk yourself through the job)
- Confusing stages and key points (stages = what has to be done; key points = how things are to be done)

- Writing key points before deciding on all the stages
- Writing key points without actually doing the stage
- Missing key points (safety points are *always* key points)
- Too many key points (beware of confusing explanatory statements with key points)
- Writing too much detail in key points (your job breakdown is for your own personal use – a simple statement which you can understand is sufficient)
- Writing key points in the wrong order (do the job yourself to check which is the correct sequence)

Practice 1

- Try to complete the job breakdown below. Note that the title states exactly what the task is. The stages have been selected, and a start has been made on the key points.

JOB BREAKDOWN

Task: Replace a spent electric light bulb

STAGES (What)	KEY POINTS (How)
1 DISCONNECT MAINS POWER	– For hanging light or wall bracket: turn appropriate mains switch to off position – For table or standard lamp: turn appropriate wall socket switch to off position; remove plug from socket
2 REMOVE SPENT BULB	– Beware hot bulb (safety point) – Hold fitting with one hand – Twist bulb anti-clockwise etc
3 CHECK WATTAGE OF SPENT BULB	
4 SELECT REPLACEMENT BULB	

5	AFFIX REPLACEMENT BULB
6	TEST REPLACEMENT BULB
7	DISPOSE OF SPENT BULB

Now make a job breakdown of your own: choose a short, simple task which you know how to do. Refer to the list of common faults if that will help you

Use

Having compiled a job breakdown, how can you make the best use of it in showing someone how to do something? Two questions which might prove useful to answer are:
- how do I make the stages clear?
- how do I emphasise the key points?

- *Stages*
Announce each stage to tell the learner what you are about to cover. Say something like 'The first thing we have to do is ...'; 'Next we have to ....'.
   Pause between stages and allow the learner time to absorb what you have just covered, before going on to the next stage. Check that the learner is up with you.

- *Key points*
   Key points can be stressed in a number of ways. We have listed them as a mnemonic (aid to memory) to help you remember them:

R	epetition
I	nflection of the voice
D	eliberate movements
E	xplanation *why*

Repetition
You often have to say things more than once, and sometimes in several different ways, for people to remember them. Do not be afraid to repeat things, especially the really important points.

Inflection of the voice
Use your voice to emphasise the key points by saying them in a stronger voice, and sometimes a bit more slowly than normal. Pause slightly after you have made an important point; it gives the point weight and allows it to sink in.

Deliberate movements
When you can do something well yourself you tend to do it very quickly. Do it at the normal speed and the poor learner will never keep up with you and might not see what you have done, or how you did it. As you demonstrate, make sure your movements are slow and deliberate enough for the learner to see and imitate. The learner can begin to speed up as (s)he gets more practised.

Explanation why
People learn much better if they understand *why* they are doing something, or completing one part of a process. This is particularly true of form filling, where inaccurate information can lead to all sorts of disasters further along the chain. People are much more likely to learn accurately if they know what an important link they are in that chain.

Use the job breakdown from the moment you start demonstrating until you have put the learner to work. Remember the job breakdown is a précis of your own thoughts – something for you to use as an instructor. Do not give it to the learner to use, unless you are happy that it is totally clear to someone else.

Giving instruction – prepare

Get everything you need to carry out your piece of instruction ready and properly arranged. Lay out the materials, equipment and any aids to instruction which you propose to use – which could be things like finished examples of the job or task in question.

Put at ease

It is no good trying to show someone how to do something if that person is uncomfortable, for whatever reason. A learner could feel ill at ease simply through being in a strange place – this could apply to new employees who have not yet become familiar with their surroundings.

If the instruction has to be given in the actual place where the job is normally performed, eg in the office or the workshop, consider how the learner might feel being instructed in front of other people. If there is a likelihood of the learner feeling self-conscious, think what arrangements could be made to make the instruction area more secluded, or pick a time when other people are not around, if that is possible. It could just be in the learner's mind that all eyes are cast in the direction of the instruction session; this is probably not the case, but you should anticipate the likely feelings of the learner.

State the job or subject

It is good practice to tell the learner in advance which particular piece of instruction is to take place. This helps to attune the learner's mind to the specific subject matter.

Obviously, just telling the learner the subject will not always be sufficient, especially if it is something completely new to the learner, when a little elaboration will be necessary.

It could be useful to indicate how this particular job or subject fits into the overall job pattern. For example, explaining the reason for completing a particular piece of paperwork in a certain way or by a specific time so that certain actions can then be done, will help the learner understand the reason why this task is necessary, as well as learning the mechanics of doing it.

If it is possible and appropriate, show the learner a model, so (s)he can see what (s)he is aiming at. It gives the learner a definite target.

Check existing knowledge

Before going into lengthy explanations of a job, find out how much the learner knows about the subject already. You might only need to teach the particular system or procedure which your organisation uses.

For example, a learner might be very well acquainted with the principles of receiving deliveries of stock from a supplier, and be alert to the need for accuracy and security. The instruction would probably just need to cover the documentation used by your business, with perhaps the identity of authorised people involved in this aspect of the job. It would be a waste of your time, and probably frustrating for the experienced learner, to be told about dock levellers, pallets and hand trucks etc.

You, of course, must be satisfied that the experience is real, and not just accept it as gospel. A little judicious questioning should soon establish the experience of your learner. You can sometimes ask a learner to show you how (s)he does something. You will very quickly see whether or not it is done correctly.

Ensure correct position

One of the critical things in showing somebody how to do something, is the relative positions of the instructor and the learner. The job and/or the equipment or machinery involved can sometimes dictate how the instruction will be given. For example, if a static piece of machinery is involved, the instructor and learner will have to adapt themselves to that. However, if hand held tools or equipment are the subject of the instruction, then the situation could be easier. Nevertheless, the instructor must ensure that the learner can view the job or task from a 'sensible' angle. For example, if the instructor shows the learner something face to face, then what the learner sees is a mirror image of the task or technique. On the other hand, if the instructor and learner stand side by side, the learner can easily get an 'operator's eye view' of the job.

Instructor's preparation

When preparing to instruct, you should always try to consider the proposed instruction from the learner's point of view, and decide whether it is suitable/comfortable etc.

Aim to give your instruction clearly and completely at a suitable pace. What pace *is* suitable will depend to some extent on the existing knowledge the learner has of the subject. As we have suggested, you should find this out before you actually begin the instruction. Using your training notes/job breakdown will help you to keep to the appropriate pace, as well as keeping you on course.

However often you have given a piece of instruction, it is useful to have your notes by you, because it is easy to overlook something, particularly if you are interrupted. When something has been left out of the sequence once, it is possible that it will never find its way back in again.

Be patient with your learner at this early stage – it will pay dividends for you both in the long run. Not everybody can pick up things at the same pace, and you must be ready to repeat or adapt your explanation or demonstration to help the learner follow what you are saying. Also bear in mind that if the learner does not understand, it could be that your explanation or demonstration is at fault.

 ## Giving instruction – instruct

Explain

The first step in the instruction cycle is to explain:
- *what* you are doing
- *how* the particular task is done, and
- *why* the job needs to be performed in that particular way or by a certain time

The reason why is often overlooked when showing someone how to do something. This is a pity, because, as we pointed out under preparation, knowing why something is done can be a great aid to learning.

There is a danger that an instructor, being familiar with the whole job, will get carried away and tell the learner the whole story in one go. This can be very confusing to the learner, who is being asked to digest too much information all at once.

In some cases, though, telling, explaining or demonstrating the whole job might be the right thing to do. For example, if you are showing someone how to operate the photocopier, it makes sense to show the whole process, and then go over it again in stages. You have to use your judgement for each learning situation.

It is important to use simple, understandable language, and vital that any jargon terms are explained to the learner. This must be a conscious effort on the part of the instructor, because when you know a job or subject well, you can easily forget that somebody coming to it new will not be familiar with all the terminology or its meaning.

Demonstrate

Having explained the job or task to the learner, you can now reinforce that explanation by demonstrating how it should be done. This is where your carefully-prepared job breakdown comes into its own. You demonstrate the job or task one stage at a time, remembering to stress those key points you identified when you drew up your job breakdown.

There are different ways of approaching this part of the instruction sequence. One is for you to demonstrate to the learner the stages of the job, emphasising the key points as you work through it, and then allow the learner to repeat what you have done.

Alternatively, you could work through the stages with the learner working alongside you and copying what you are doing; once again you will emphasise the key points as you come to them.

Which method is the more suitable will depend on the job, or the stage you have reached, and the knowledge and ability of your learner.

Do not hesitate to repeat your demonstration and explanation as many times as appropriate. Once again, patience in this early stage will be much welcomed by your learner.

We said earlier that a learner cannot normally do a practical job initially at the speed of an experienced worker, and the instructor needs to slow down so that the learner can see what is happening. For some jobs, particularly those requiring manual dexterity, like sharpening a knife on a steel or drawing a cork from a bottle with a corkscrew, the demonstration should not be slowed down too much. This is because doing that particular job at a slower speed requires slightly different skills from those which you are trying to teach.

Demonstrate at a slower speed where appropriate to show detail, perhaps of a key point, and then at the proper speed, to illustrate the actual technique in action.

Where demonstrating at other than full speed would be difficult (eg you cannot toss a pancake in slow motion), consider the use of video, when the task or stage done at the correct speed can be slowed down when played back to the learner to illustrate the technique, rather like a television programme will do, for example, to show the action of a bird in flight.

Try out

This is where you allow your learner to demonstrate the job or stage back to you. Where appropriate, allow the learner to complete the job or stage, which you can then discuss together afterwards, and establish where things went wrong – if they did! Do remember that however badly the job turned out at this first attempt, start by praising the learner for the bit that went right. It is very necessary to try to stimulate confidence in the learner at this point in the instruction cycle.

Where a high degree of safety is involved in the task being demonstrated, you should stop the activity at once if it is going wrong, and not allow the learner to continue as suggested above. Remember that safety is *always* a key point, and stopping a demonstration on safety grounds will help to emphasise that point to the learner.

Check that the learner understands the job or stage. You can do this by asking suitable questions. 'Do you understand?' is *not* a suitable question! (see Chapter 6 – Talking to Customers or Clients on the effective use of questions).

Possibly a better idea is to ask the learner to explain the job or subject by talking through it as it is being done. This will not only help to underline to the learner and to you that the job or subject is understood, it can also help to cover up the (often) embarrassing silence while you stand looking at the demonstration.

If the job involved is a sitting down one, try not to loom over the learner while the job is being done. This could be very distracting, not to say intimidating, for the learner.

Correct

We have already touched on the importance of praise to the learner. Cultivating confidence in the ability to do the job is helped considerably by your attitude at this stage. Begin your comments on a positive note, and then develop them to cover the areas which need improvement. Assure the learner that it is normal practice to work up to Experienced Worker Standard (EWS), and very rarely is it achieved at the first attempt.

Repeat the instruction and demonstration cycle as appropriate. Remember the importance of your attitude if the job or stage was not done right the first, or even the second, time.

Giving instruction – put to work

Having given the appropriate amount of instruction, you need to allow the learner to do the job for real. It is important that the learner knows the extent of the job responsibilities: in other words, where the job itself begins and where it ends. For example, whether the 'raw materials' for the job, whatever form they take, are supplied to the job location, or whether they have to be collected from somewhere else by the job holder. When the job is completed, does the job holder take them on to the next stage, or are they collected from where the job has just been performed? It is necessary for the learner to be aware of these facts rights from the start.

It is probable that your own job responsibilities will take you away from the place where you have just been instructing. Do not leave your learner stranded, but point out and name the person who will provide help in these early stages of doing the job. Be sure to let this person know that you are going to be doing this: better still, introduce them to each other.

Encourage the learner to ask questions, either of you or the person you have designated to help. This is better than letting the learner struggle on unsupervised and feeling abandoned.

Giving instruction – check

Your responsibilities still have not entirely finished. Remember to follow up the progress your learner is making, giving praise and encouragement as appropriate. This need not be over-elaborate; the fact that you are taking the trouble to acknowledge the learner and the work being done will make no small contribution to the standard, as well as probably the volume, of work being produced by your ex-learner.

This might seem a very long-winded way of showing someone how to do something, but each step can be very short for a simple task. The way you prepare and present the job to the learner has a great effect on how well and quickly the learner learns. The way you present yourself is an important part of this process.

Practice 2

- Choose a simple task which you know how to do well. It could be something at home or at work like tying a Windsor knot in a necktie, using a fax machine, applying eye makeup, mending a puncture etc.
- Make your instruction notes in the form of a job breakdown (refer to Practice 1).

- Find someone willing to learn, who has not done the job before or who has little experience of it; you might like to tell this person that you are trying out your skills as an instructor.
- Show the person how to do the job, remembering to go through *all* the steps shown in the instruction sequence. See Points to remember at the end of this chapter.
- Ask your volunteer–learner to help you analyse what you did well and where you went wrong.

Points to remember from this chapter

- Do not try to teach something you cannot do yourself
- Prepare your notes as a job breakdown
- When you are emphasising key points, remember:

R	epetition
I	inflection
D	eliberate movements
E	xplanation *why*

- Follow the plan outlined on page 93: keep it by you and use it whenever you are planning to show someone how to do something. You can then be sure that your instruction is given in a logical sequence and that nothing is left out.
- Remember, do not be afraid to repeat the instruction cycle if you feel it is necessary. Continue until the learner has reached the standard you require.

PREPARE
- put at ease
- state the job or subject
- check existing knowledge
- ensure correct position

1 EXPLAIN
- what, how, why

2 DEMONSTRATE
- one stage at a time

4 CORRECT
- check full
  understanding

3 TRY OUT
- learner demonstrates
  and explains

PUT TO WORK
- indicate job responsibility
- name person who will help
- encourage questions

CHECK AS NECESSARY
- follow up progress
- give encouragement

[Based on: Training Services Agency,
Training within Industry, Job Instruction
and Communication, TAS CI]

9 In a Formal Meeting

In this chapter:
- You have a contribution to make
- Preparation, including agendas and minutes
- Arriving at the meeting
- Being a member of the meeting
  - the conduct of the meeting
  - your body language
  - making your point
  - personalities
  - some tricks of the trade
  - group decisions
- After the meeting
- Formal presentations at meetings

 ## You have a contribution to make

This chapter is about presenting yourself and your point of view in meetings – meetings of any sort. They could be very informal (perhaps a meeting with friends planning an outing); they could be formal meetings outside work, school or college (the sports club, the photographic society etc); they could be formal business meetings called committees, sub-committees, working parties, project teams etc. They are all meetings attended by a small number of people (up to about 12), not large gatherings, where your contribution would have to be made in a very different way (see Chapter 11 – In Front of a Group of People).

Whether you have been asked to join a meeting in an informal way, or whether you have been formally elected or appointed, you are there for a purpose. You have a contribution to make, no matter how inexperienced or experienced you are. Inexperienced people often have fresh ideas, which are worth listening to; more mature people can help clarify, guide and put forward new ideas themselves. Age is no barrier to being a good meeting person.

You cannot really practise being a member of a meeting without actually being in a meeting, so this chapter has no Practice sections. It is intended as a guide, with practical hints, for people who have, perhaps, to attend a meeting for the first time, or for people who would like a little help on how to present themselves and conduct themselves at meetings. It is very frustrating to come away from a meeting without having made the points you wanted to make.

Preparation, including agendas and minutes

As with everything else, good preparation for a meeting helps a lot.

You should be sent, well beforehand, a record of what was agreed at the previous meeting (the Minutes), an Agenda of what is to be discussed at the coming meeting, and any backup papers necessary. It is not very satisfactory to read all these papers on the way to the meeting; if you are going to make a contribution of any value, you need to study the papers well beforehand so that you know roughly what is likely to be said and what your thoughts on the matter are. It will also give you time to prepare any papers or collect any facts you want to take to the meeting yourself.

Documents

The formal documents which normally go with a meeting are:
● Notice of Meeting
● Agenda
● Minutes of Previous Meeting

Notice of Meeting
This is just a formal, written notice telling you when and where the meeting is to be held. Sometimes the rules of the club, society or company require a formal notice to be sent out at a certain time, say one month or two weeks before the meeting is due to be held, but that is normally for very formal meetings, such as an Annual General Meeting.

All you have to do with a Notice of Meeting is to make sure you know the time, date and venue, and that you can attend. If you cannot, let the Secretary, or whoever has sent the Notice, know – you should send your apologies for being absent.

Agenda
This is the list of items to be discussed at the meeting. It usually starts with:

1 Apologies for absence (this is where your formal apology is normally read)
2 Minutes of Previous Meeting (these are agreed and signed – see below)
3 Matters Arising (these are short matters arising from the previous meeting which can be quickly cleared up and are not part of the main Agenda items)
4
5   (main items to be discussed)
6 etc

Two final items are normally:

- Date of Next Meeting (it is wise to fix the date then and there)
- AOB (Any Other Business, where members can bring up any topic not covered in the Main Agenda items)

Usually the person running the meeting (the Chairman, Chairwoman, Chairperson or Chair) will work through the items in order so that nothing gets left out.

Minutes of Previous Meeting
The Minutes of a meeting are the formal record of the discussions which took place and the action agreed – the word Minutes means *minutiae*, or detail, and has nothing to do with time.

The Minutes are usually written by the Secretary and agreed with the Chair before being sent out to Members. When you come to read the Minutes and you find something which you know is wrong, you should:
- let the Secretary know *before* the next meeting
- make sure it gets altered *at* the next meeting, when you get to that item (Minutes of Previous Meeting) on the agenda

The Minutes are a record of what was actually said, not what anyone thought should or should not have been said, so you can only alter something which you know with certainty was wrongly recorded. If it is wrong, do not let it pass – have the courage to point it out.

Once the Minutes have been agreed by everyone – often by a show of hands – they will be signed by the Chair as an official record of the Meeting, and cannot be altered after that.

Lobbying

To 'lobby' someone is to chat to them before the meeting, find out what they think about certain subjects and if necessary make sure they are on your side. It is called lobbying because it is the sort of persuasion that goes on in the 'lobbies' or entrance rooms in the Houses of Parliament where people go to 'lobby' or persuade their MPs. It is the sort of thing you see going on before Board Meetings in TV soaps.

There is no harm in finding out what people think before a meeting, and it can be quite useful to do so. You need to be aware of when people are lobbying you, and be careful not to agree to a certain line before you have heard all the arguments; there is nothing to stop you changing your mind in the meeting anyway.

If you are due to attend a meeting (with others from your company) with a client, agreeing tactics and points of view before the meeting is important, so that you show a united front to the client. This is not lobbying, but briefing, and you usually have a de-briefing after the meeting to agree action from then on.

Action

You need to check before the meeting that you have done everything you promised to do at the previous meeting. Sometimes Minutes have an Action column on the right-hand side, with the initials of the people who have agreed to do certain things. Do not rely totally on the Minutes, though. You need to make a note yourself of the things you have agreed to do; use the Minutes as a final check.

☐ *Preparation checklist*

- Note the day, time and place of the Meeting
- Apologise if you cannot attend
- Let the Secretary have copies of any papers you want sent out before the Meeting
- Read the Minutes and let the Secretary know if anything is wrong
- Read the Agenda and any other papers

- Check you have done everything you agreed to do
- Prepare any papers etc you need to take to the Meeting with sufficient copies for everyone
- Take your diary with you

 Arriving at the meeting

If you are attending a meeting for the first time, it is useful to arrive about five minutes early – not too early, so that you will feel embarrassed, nor just on time or late. Five minutes will give you time to find where to sit, sort your papers out and be ready for the meeting to begin.

Where should you sit? If it is a formal meeting with name cards or name plates already set out, you have no problem. If not, do not sit at the head of the table, where the Chair will sit, nor immediately to the left or right of that, where the Secretary will probably sit. If you sit at the foot of the table you might feel a bit exposed, so try to sit along one of the sides. If the table is round, just do not sit where others have put their papers.

What should you wear and what should be your image? It depends, of course, on what sort of meeting it is, but a meeting is called to do business of some sort, so unless it is a very informal affair, outside work, you should wear something reasonably smart and formal. You will perhaps not want to be too conspicuous at a first meeting, so do not wear anything too way out. Your papers will look better in a bag or briefcase rather than in an envelope or a plastic bag. Remember to take something to write with, and something to write on, although many people make their notes on their Agendas.

Greet people as you arrive – say hello, good morning or whatever. If a secretary is showing you in, remember to greet him or her, too. (In this case we are talking about a personal secretary, not the Secretary to the Meeting, although they may be the same person.)

Try to find out the personal secretary's name, remember it and use it. It is polite to do this anyway, but also you may find you need his or her help in the future if you are late, have lost papers or something.

Arrival checklist

- Arrive five minutes early
- Greet others, including the personal secretary
- Wear something a little formal
- Carry your papers in a briefcase or bag
- Bring something to make notes with
- Choose your seat carefully

Being a member of the meeting

To get the most out of the meeting for yourself, and also to make the best contribution you can, there are several things to consider:

The conduct of the meeting

If everyone starts speaking at once, nobody hears what is going on and a great deal of time is wasted. Therefore a good Chair (see Chapter 10 – Chairing a Discussion Group) will normally go through the Agenda items in sequence, letting anyone who wants to speak do so and generally keeping control of the meeting. It is often customary to speak 'through the Chair', as they say. That is, everyone addresses their remarks to the Chair so that private conversations do not develop and everyone can hear what is said. This may seem a strange way of going about things, but it actually works quite well, particularly in a slightly larger meeting of, say, a dozen people.

If you have something to say on a particular point, make sure you catch the Chair's eye by leaning forward, looking directly at the Chair and making a sign with your hand – a raised finger is enough. Alternatively you can say 'Mr Chairman' or 'Madam Chairman' or 'Bob' or 'Mrs Bates', or whatever the convention is for that meeting. Watch, and see what the others do. In any case, do not interrupt: just indicate to the Chair, and you will be given your chance to speak.

At a first meeting there may be several things you know little about or do not understand, particularly if you are a new member coming into a group which has been meeting regularly for some time. At first it is better to watch and listen, but if there is a point which you really do not understand and need to know about, ask the Chair to explain it for you. No-one will mind, if you are new.

Your body language

As we said in Chapter 1 – Body Language, other people can tell a lot about you from the way you sit in a group. So do not position your chair outside the group, nor with your back to anyone; re-position it if necessary. Do not look too laid-back either – it looks rather arrogant at a first meeting.

Do not fidget or fiddle with pens, paperclips etc, even if you do find the meeting boring – and meetings can be extremely boring if they are not well run. It does not look too good to spend the whole meeting doodling, either.

Making your point

When you have something to say, say it as clearly and concisely as possible. Make sure everyone can hear what you are saying – take account of traffic noise, rattling cups etc.

Speak 'to the Chair', but look at everyone else in the meeting from time to time. If you do not look at them, you will not know what their reactions are. Are they looking at you in an interested way? Have they pushed their chairs back, folded their arms and started looking elsewhere? If so, they are probably not interested in what you are saying, or they might even be hostile, and you will need to win them round. Do they keep looking at their watches? If so, they are probably wanting their tea or something, so you need to get on with it.

If you want to 'table' any papers (that is, put them on the table at the meeting, rather than sending them out beforehand), give them to the members of the meeting at the time you want them to consider them or right at the start of the meeting. In any case, give people time to read through them quickly, indicate which are the important points for the meeting, and what can be better read afterwards. People very often want to read what you give them then and there.

If you have a particularly strong accent, or if there is someone at the meeting who will find it difficult to understand you for some reason, speak fairly slowly and make sure your diction is clear (see Chapter 3 – Oral Assessment).

The Chair should make you keep to the point, but you can help by being very clear about the points you want to make, making them and then shutting up. Do not let yourself get side-tracked, nor drawn into discussing details which can be settled outside the meeting.

Personalities

Here again the Chair should control the meeting, so that there is no great clash of personalities, but you can help.

Leave personal feelings outside the meeting room, and listen to other people's arguments with your ears and brain, not your heart. It is quite difficult to listen objectively to people you do not like, but the facts and opinions they put forward are valuable, and you ought to be adult enough to take account of them.

On the other hand, it might be quite wrong to back someone up just because you are very good friends; their opinions could be way out of line on certain things, and you need to be able to recognise when that is so.

Some tricks of the trade

There are one or two things you sometimes need to be aware of.

When there has been a 'natural break', for refreshments, perhaps, watch out for distinct changes of attitude after visits to the ladies or gents. More things are decided in these informal meetings than many people are aware of.

Watch out for people pushing through ideas at the last minute, probably towards the end of the meeting when time is getting short and you are into AOB. If you suddenly become aware that someone is raising an important issue and trying to get it agreed without much discussion, ask for it to be put on the Agenda for the next meeting. As a member of that meeting you have the right to have time to consider it properly.

If items are discussed and no decision taken because the meeting moved on (normally accidentally but sometimes deliberately), remind the Chair that the decision has got to be made. It is better to put the blame on yourself, and say something like, 'I'm sorry, I must have missed it, but I'm not quite sure what we agreed there', rather saying, 'You've forgotten that point, can we go back to it?'.

Greet the person who brings the refreshments or clears away. It is only good manners to say thank you, but, on a more cynical level, you can be sure of being well looked after next time.

Group decisions

Meetings are called to discuss topics and make decisions, and nine times out of ten a group decision is arrived at.

To get to the decision the meeting might have gone through arguments, conflict, disagreement and a certain amount of in-fighting, but in the end the decision is the group's. How they got there is no-one's business but theirs. What went on in the meeting should not normally be discussed outside the meeting, unless there is good reason to do so – a de-briefing, for example, which might involve passing on thoughts and decisions to others.

Sometimes people cannot agree about something and a vote is taken. The majority vote wins the day, and then all members of the meeting must stick by the decision, whether they like it or not – that is what democracy is all about.

If the meeting takes a decision which you are dead against, you have three options:

- support it
- try to get it reversed at a future meeting
- resign from the group

What you must not do is undermine the decision outside the meeting while still being a member of the group. It is a hard pill to swallow sometimes. This sort of thing does not happen very often, so it is not something you should worry about.

Member's checklist

- Don't interrupt; make your points through the Chair
- Ask, if you do not understand
- Position your chair correctly
- Watch your body language
- Make your points clearly and concisely
- Make sure you can be heard and understood
- Watch other people's reactions
- Use handouts properly
- Leave feelings outside
- Be aware of what is going on
- Thank the refreshment people
- Stand by group decisions

After the meeting

There are three, or possibly four, main things for you to do when the meeting is over:

- Take all your papers away with you, particularly anything which is confidential
- Update any other diaries you keep
- Do whatever you agreed to do personally
- Report back or de-brief, if that is part of your job

The meeting is not properly finished until you have done all these things.

You could well find that being a member of a committee or group entails quite a lot of work outside the meetings, and you must be prepared to do this if you are to be a valuable (and valued) group member.

You might also have to report back to or de-brief colleagues. This can sometimes be done through your own written report or newsletter, or you might need to run a mini-meeting of your own. People who are not members of the committee or group will not normally see the Minutes of the meetings, so it is up to you to pass on the decisions, messages and thoughts. You have to draw a line here between reporting what went on and gossiping about what was said and who said what. It is generally better to stick to the facts.

 After the meeting checklist

- Take everything away
- Update other diaries
- Do what you said you would
- Report back, if appropriate

Formal presentations at meetings

Sometimes you might be co-opted or invited to attend a meeting to make a formal presentation – a sales pitch, for example. In this case you can follow much of what is said in Chapter 11 – In Front of a Group of People. The main difference is that you are not in control of the meeting, you just have a 'spot' within someone else's meeting – which could be run by a senior person within the organisation. Check before the meeting whether you are to attend the whole meeting or only part of it.

When making your preparations, first establish clearly in your own mind certain relevant facts:

- why is the meeting being held?
- why am I being asked to participate in it?
- what *exactly* am I expected to contribute?
- how can I ensure that I do not overlap with other people's material, and vice versa?
- how long am I being given to make my presentation, and will I be allowed to keep to it?
- what do I want to get out of the meeting?

It is vital to ensure that you have precise terms of reference, and that you keep your preparation within your brief. At the same time you must keep in your mind who you will be addressing at the meeting, and their status within the organisation and in relation to you. Follow the suggestions for preparation covered in Chapter 11 – In Front of a Group of People: you will find that they will work quite well for this type of situation. Ensure that you have all your facts and figures readily to hand, because unlike the sort of formal presentation covered in Chapter 11, the aftermath is likely to be more 'lively'.

Explain at the beginning of your presentation when you would like questions to be taken. Preferably allow time at the end for this. If you find yourself subjected to hostile questioning, do not allow yourself to be intimidated or swayed. If it is an in-company/internal meeting, you might know the *reason* behind a hostile question, which might not be to do with the subject in hand at all.

You can only defend your corner if you know your subject thoroughly, and have done your homework. Defending your point of view does not necessarily mean being defensive about your subject. In this situation you will probably need a certain amount of flexibility, which can only come about, once again, through a knowledge of your subject. You will be able to respond to different aspects of your subject with authority and confidence.

What you say must be factual and illustrate your point of view in a way which supports your main argument. However strong your feelings about your subject, keep your emotions under control – particularly in the face of adversity.

Avoid making your most important points in your opening statement, although there is nothing to stop you making a 'dramatic' statement to make your listeners sit up and pay attention. Think about your important points while doing your preparation, and suitable moments will become apparent. Do not make these points all together; give your listeners time to digest one point before throwing the next one at them. However, do make sure the group realises that they *are* important points when you make them! Without detracting from your main message, try to keep a little something up your sleeve, particularly for when answering questions.

It is dangerous to assume that people, even from within the same organisation, have the same degree of knowledge as you do: they may have more, they may have less. In any case you will never get your message across effectively if you fail to show any interest or enthusiasm for your subject matter, which might happen if it is something you have been 'volunteered' into doing.

The visual aids mentioned in Chapter 11 – In Front of a Group of People, can also be used in this type of meeting. If you prepare and use them well, they will give added weight and authority to your presentation.

Give consideration to what you will wear: something suitable for the occasion. Your material/message is the 'star', so do not wear anything which detracts from that. Pay attention to your posture; the way you stand or sit, and utilise the controlled use of gesture to your advantage. Maintain eye contact with the group; do not avoid the gaze of the senior person. Match your body language to the words; remember you are presenting a visual image to the group as well as a verbal one, so make sure they are compatible (see Chapter 1 – Body Language, for help in some of these areas).

☐ *Formal presentation checklist*

- Establish ground rules of meeting
- Know your objectives and your audience
- Prepare thoroughly, including visual aids
- Defend your corner with logical argument, not emotion
- Consider your appearance and body language

As we said right at the beginning of this chapter, the only way to practise being a member of a meeting and to develop your self presentation skills at meetings is to attend them.

When you do attend meetings, use this chapter as a checklist for your preparation and to analyse afterwards how well you got on. The final list of points to remember will help you.

Points to remember from this chapter

Remember these key points by answering these questions after your meeting:
- How much of a contribution did you make to the meeting?
- Had you done all the preparation you should?
- Did you sit in the right place?
- What was your body language like?
- Did you understand all that was going on?
  - If not, will it be better next time?
- Did you ask for explanations when you needed to?
- Did you manage to make all the points you wanted to?
- How did other people react to what you had to say?
- Did you remember to thank the refreshment people?
- Were there any decisions made that you have got to do something about?
- Did you bring all your papers away with you?
- Have you updated your other diaries?
- Have you got to report back to anyone?
- What did you agree to do between meetings?
- Is there anything you have to get to the Secretary to send out with the next Notice of Meeting?
- Are you looking forward to the next one?!
- If you were making a formal presentation, did you achieve your objectives?
  - If not, why not?

10 Chairing a Discussion Group

In this chapter:
- You as group leader
- Preparation
- Introduction
- Controlling the discussion:
  - listening, observing, thinking
  - summaries
  - handling people
    - the silent person, the dominant personality, the 'expert', the 'happy wanderer', the 'bee keeper'

You as group leader

As with any sort of leadership activities, your personality and behaviour will have an influence on the group you are leading, which on this occasion is a discussion group or meeting. Your self presentation will need to include the physical posture you adopt for the discussion, which is just as important when sitting as when standing (see Chapter 1 – Body Language). Look alert and interested; be careful not to lean forward in an aggressive and dominant way. Make sure you look open and responsive.

Gesture can be very effective in controlling a discussion, to ensure those who wish to participate do so, and to encourage the hesitant ones.

Holding up your hand like this, palm towards the speaker, says, 'Please don't speak yet, wait your turn.'

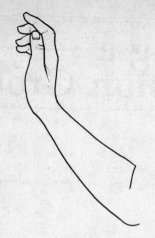

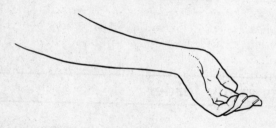

Your hand held like this invites someone to speak.

Eye contact with the group needs to be constant to interpret the various moods of the individuals. However great your enthusiasm for the subject, you must remain impartial in controlling the discussion, because your overall responsibility is to serve the group and refrain from the temptation to dominate the meeting.

Preparation

Seating arrangements are important for successful discussion meetings. Seat the members of the group so that they can see each other, and you. Make sure each person is physically comfortable. If it is a formal meeting, with several papers, it is usually better to sit round a table. Informal meetings can do away with this barrier.

Anyone taking notes or Minutes should sit beside you so that the two of you can communicate easily. Other members of the group will probably sort themselves out, but try not to let 'enemies' sit opposite each other in a confrontational way or quiet people get lost at the far end of the group.

Introduction

Once the group is assembled you must give the lead. Introduce the general purpose of the meeting, and state the initial topic. It is often useful to write it up, perhaps on a flipboard, where everyone can read it – unless it is already written out on an agenda. If you are using an agenda, you must keep to it.

Work out your introductory statement in advance; read it out to the group if necessary, to help ensure that you set the scene adequately to help the group members all get onto the same wavelength. Your introduction will help to make the participants into a group from being a collection of individuals, through having a common interest in the subject to be discussed. Your formal introductory statement should conclude with a well-phrased question, as a means of getting the discussion under way.

Be prepared for, and not put off by, the pause which might follow your opening question. The group will be thinking about the content of your introductory statement and the significance of your question. After what might seem an age to you, somebody will break the silence, even if it is not a direct response to your question. This does not matter, because once that initial silence has been broken, you will find that group members will begin to contribute.

Controlling the discussion

As the discussion paper gets under way, you, in your role as leader, need to call on your techniques of control. This will involve you in listening, observing and thinking (LOT) about what is happening around the table or circle.

Listening

Listening is an active not a passive role, and, as part of leading a discussion group, often involves deciding what is really meant behind the words actually being said: this will be influenced by how articulate the group members are. Quite a lot of the time be prepared to interpret what is said, or help group members to express their thoughts clearly and logically.

Observing

Part of your time should be spent observing those members of the group who are not speaking or contributing to the discussion. Consider how they are reacting to those who are speaking: their body language could tell you a lot (refer to Chapter 1 – Body Language). You need to watch for the moment when the silent, passive or reluctant member has something to say. If you fail to notice the signs – for example, an intake of breath, opening the mouth, looking at you in a positive way – you may have lost the moment for ever, and perhaps the chance to hear what could have been a very valuable contribution to the discussion.

Thinking

Thinking is valuable to the leader of a group discussion. You need to be able to consider objectively the implications of what is being said, and of the attitudes of other group members to those statements or views (the body language signals again). You may need to make the odd statement yourself, or ask a question, to help clarify a particular point. Clarifying helps you to think straight, and helps the other group members as well.

Summaries

It is part of your function as the leader of a group discussion to keep the group up-to-date with what has been covered. This will probably take the form of intermediate summaries. Your aim should be to obtain agreement from the group members, and then move on to the next topic or subject on the agenda. A short summary after each point is a great help to the note-takers or the Minute taker.

Handling people

As a leader of a group discussion you need to be able to handle the different types of people in that group, bearing in mind that people are individuals with different personalities. Everyone must feel involved, and some must not be allowed to dominate the discussion at the expense of the others. You must be prepared to deal with conflict within the group. The important point is not to let it get out of hand. Try to establish the *real* reason for any discord, and attempt to resolve it. It is better to get the conflict out in the open than to let it simmer.

It is useful for a leader of a discussion group personally to be able to sort out what is fact and what is opinion; help the group to identify or establish the facts from information being given by a group member. It could lead into dangerous ground if a group carries on discussing opinions as though they were facts. Opinion is valuable in a discussion, particularly if it is well-formed, or based on experience. A person should be able to support opinions with facts.

Any group is composed of individuals. They may be gathered together under a common identity; the Health & Safety Committee, the Policy Advisory Group, or similar, but underneath they are all individuals with their own unique personalities, wishing to express – not to say sometimes impose – their own views and opinions. Your role as a leader in this situation is to see that they are able to do that, but without detriment to one another or the aims of the group as a whole – or, indeed, the subject under discussion.

This means that you need to be aware of the different types likely to be encountered within a typical group, and be prepared to handle them effectively, for the benefit of the group as a whole. You can only really practise handling people in the live situation, but we hope these few comments will help to point you in the right direction.

A typical group could comprise, in varying degrees:
- the silent person
- the dominant personality
- the 'expert'
- the 'happy wanderer'
- the 'bee keeper'

The silent person

It is easy to dismiss in one's mind someone within a meeting or discussion group who does not seem to be participating as much as the others. In fact, as the leader, it could be easy to overlook that person if your attention is fully taken up with those who *are* involved; particularly if things are going well, or the pace is hotting up.

Consider for a moment why someone within a discussion group is remaining silent while others are holding forth. There could be several reasons:

- not familiar with the subject
- could genuinely feel there is nothing to contribute
- hesitant to speak in front of others – perhaps of senior rank within the organisation, if it is an in-company meeting
- has had previous contributions not taken seriously
- thinking about what others are saying before making a considered contribution

How could you as the leader decide which of these, or other, reasons apply to the silent person within your group? A little interpretation of that person's body language could help: try to glean what information you can (refer again to Chapter 1 – Body Language for guidance).

Feedback is really the key, but above all try not to miss the moment when the silent person is ready to contribute. To ask straight out at the wrong moment could stifle the chance of hearing any views from that person. To acknowledge the positive sign and ensure that the person is given the chance to speak at the right moment, could mean that something very significant is added to the discussion. Do not underestimate the silent or quiet person.

The dominant personality

Some people by their very presence can dominate a discussion meeting. This might be because of their status in relation to other members of the group, their style of managing or organising other people anyway in their normal place of work, or, sometimes, their sheer physical size.

As the leader of a discussion group, it is important that you do not allow your authority to be eroded by the dominance of the personality of a member of your group. This does not mean that you have to try and 'top' the other personality all the time: this could make things unbearable for the remainder of the group, especially if your own personality is inclined towards the formidable.

One danger of the dominant personality is that the less-strongminded members of your group could be swayed into following the path proposed by that personality. There could always be a feeling of frustration or resentment if the discussion group leader does not allow the opportunity for the free participation of the others, through being unable to stem the tide of opinion from the strong personality.

Your problem then, as leader of the group, is when and how to stop the floodtide to allow others the opportunity to contribute, but without offending the owner of that dominant personality – who may not realise quite how oppressive it is.

The key to a possible solution is breathing space. However much the dominant person may appear to be able to say without pausing for breath, there will be an occasion when this is necessary. This is your cue to get in with a quick 'Thank you', probably accompanied by a slight gesture of the hand, like a policeman stopping the flow of traffic, as mentioned earlier, 'perhaps we could hear what other members think' – or something to that effect. You have to be quick, however, otherwise the floodgates will be open again. You will no doubt be rewarded by ample contributions from the remaining, grateful, members of the group.

All this does not mean that the person with the dominant personality cannot make a valuable contribution to the discussion; it is just that it needs to be kept in proportion.

The 'expert'

This heading has been deliberately written in inverted commas. The real and acknowledged expert can contribute a lot of value to a group discussion, and should be welcomed by you, as leader. Quite often this sort of expert can be invited into a meeting for the specific purpose of providing the group with some useful or essential background material to aid its discussions – the sort of situation we covered in the last part of Chapter 9 – In a Formal Meeting, where you might be that expert. It could be that this expert would leave the group after the factual material had been presented, and perhaps answered a few questions.

Our 'expert' on the other hand could be the self-appointed sort: the person who has probably some working knowledge of the subject, but who could not, by any normal standards, be considered an expert on the subject. The danger here is that the group may accept the opinions of this 'expert' as being the generally-accepted views of those involved with that particular subject.

As leader, it should be part of your function to expect any alleged 'expert' contribution to be backed up with facts. Do a little probing on behalf of the group.

Do not belittle the contribution made by this type of 'expert'. The fact of having some sort of practical involvement in the subject matter could stand this group member apart from the rest of the participants, but, as leader, you should beware of letting your group accept everything at its face value.

The 'happy wanderer'

We must all at some time have been involved in group discussion meetings with the person who is more than happy to talk about anything rather than the subject in hand. Very often these 'asides' can be very interesting or amusing, but they may not have anything substantial to contribute to the subject of the discussion.

Particularly where the meeting time, or the time of some of the group members, is limited, you, as the discussion leader, have an important role in ensuring that what time *is* available is used to full advantage, and for the benefit of the purpose of the meeting.

There are often occasions within a contribution by a member of the group where an illustration or an account of an incident is appropriate. In your capacity as discussion leader, you must make sure that a relative or supportive example does not get developed into something irrelevant to the immediate subject under discussion.

This can often come about by another member of the group asking a supplementary question, perhaps through curiosity about what happened after the illustrated incident. You, as leader, must make sure that your group does not get led away from the main point of the illustration into irrelevant areas.

Make a simple comment like, 'Perhaps you could continue/explore that further after the meeting/over coffee'. This must be done with quiet authority, but in a way which does not offend or frustrate the person giving the illustration, or the group. Your job as leader is to keep your group on the right track, within the constraints of time, and not allow members to wander off into vague areas which do not serve the objectives of the discussion meeting.

The 'bee-keeper'

To have a bee in one's bonnet is defined as being obsessed about some matter, especially a matter to which one is opposed. There are those 'bee keepers' who find the opportunity at any discussion meeting, whatever the official subject matter may be, to produce from their bonnet the current obsession.

Group leaders beware: these 'bees' can be great discussion killers, especially if the group has heard it all before. This is definitely a situation for you to don your group leader's velvet glove. You have got to be firm in not allowing the particular 'gripe', which may have a relevance to the matter under discussion – but not always –, to detract from the general and open discussion.

This can prove quite a challenge to a discussion group leader, if the 'bee keeper' is also the dominant personality in the group. But we have never said that being the leader of a discussion group is easy!

The key to this situation, once again, is not to let the matter get out of hand or out of proportion. By all means let the 'bees' out of the bonnet for an airing, but then they should be safely put away, to allow the rest of the group to contribute to the official discussion.

You might be tempted to impose your leader's authority and, perhaps being aware of the 'bee keeper' among your group, determine to keep the obsession under cover. Consider carefully the effects of this if you decide to go ahead. You could make an enemy of your 'bee keeper', who will be equally determined for the current obsession to be aired. If denied this opportunity (s)he could decide not to contribute to the meeting at all. A member of a discussion group obviously opting out is bound to have an effect on the remaining members, and you will find it very difficult to get a good and open discussion going if there is an 'atmosphere' over the meeting.

Once again tact, firmness, fairness – laced with a touch of humour – can help you to keep your discussion on the right track.

You can probably think of other types of personality which can be met in discussion groups, not included in these notes. We have not attempted to cover every situation, but simply to give a flavour of the variety of individual characters you are likely to encounter as a leader of a discussion group.

If you are currently a member of discussion groups, rather than a leader, consciously try to identify the types of your fellow members – remember to include yourself(!) – and take note of how other leaders handle those different individuals: you can learn a lot from observing others. A discussion group looks a lot different from the leader's chair, and in the end you will only learn the skills of being a discussion group leader by actually doing it in a real situation.

We hope this chapter has not put you off the idea, but at least alerted you to some of the pitfalls. If you use all your skills – the LOT – you will find it very tiring to lead a discussion group or meeting, but it is very satisfying to do it well.

116

Points to remember from this chapter

- You are there to serve the group not dominate it
- Be aware of your own body language
- Prepare: think about the seating
    know how you are going start off
- Introduce the subject effectively
- Listen, Observe and Think (LOT)
- Clarify and summarise
- Stick to the agenda, if there is one
- Control the meeting and the people so that everyone has a chance to contribute

11 In Front of a Group of People

In this chapter:
- Preparation of material
- Presentation area
  - seating
  - lighting
  - heating and ventilation
  - noise
- Presentation
  - Poise
  - Pace
  - Pitch
- Feedback
- After sales service
- Discussion
- Visual aids
- Post mortem

Preparation of material

A formal presentation in front of a group of people is a well-tried method of imparting knowledge. It can be a very useful means of introducing a new subject, particularly where all the detail need not be remembered. The success or failure of this method depends almost entirely on the presentation skills of the person standing in front of the group of people.

As with most things, there are advantages and disadvantages of this method:

- *Advantages:* the detail of what is going to be said and the way in which the material is going to be presented can be carefully worked out in advance.
- *Disadvantages:* the members of the group do not have to give evidence of accepting what is being presented to them. They may look attentive, but how much is actually being absorbed?

The first step you need to take when starting to prepare the material for your presentation is to be able to give positive answers to the following questions:

- Do I know my subject?
- Are my terms of reference clear in my own mind?

Until you can answer 'yes' to both those questions, proceed no further in trying to prepare your presentation material. You must make sure that you understand what you are going to talk about before you start, because if you do not understand it, none of your listeners will – in fact they might soon become non-listeners, when they realise you are in the dark too.

When you have yourself sorted out, you can begin to think about the group to whom your presentation will be made. Do this by trying to answer some more questions:

- What is the composition of the group?
- At what level should I pitch the content of my presentation?
- Why does the group need the information I am to present?
- What is it *essential* that the group remembers at the end of my presentation? – so, which major points do I need to emphasise?
- How can I best ensure that my message gets across?
- Should I distribute a handout in advance?
- Should I use charts, diagrams or actual examples during my presentation to help the group understand my message more easily?

Clarifying the answers to these and similar questions will help you to decide how you should set about the preparation of your material.

A useful first step is to break down the content of your presentation into manageable sections, and sort them into the most appropriate order, so that your material can be presented in a logical sequence. This sounds obvious, but the logical sequence is not always apparent at first sight. Try using a separate sheet of paper for each subject or section; they can then easily be shuffled into the correct order when you decide which is the most suitable sequence – this can save a lot of re-writing.

Naturally, your material will have an introduction, a middle or explanatory section and a conclusion. We recommend that your *introduction* is written out in full. This will help you to get your presentation under way in the way you have planned. It will also help you to gain confidence, especially if this is one of your early experiences of being in front of a group of people.

For your *middle or explanatory section* you should only need headings or short statements (key points), because you will have made sure that you know your subject, and you just need a form of checklist to help keep you on the right track, and to make sure that you do not overlook anything in the excitement of the moment.

You *conclusion*, we suggest, is also written out in full. This will help you to make sure that you get over your final points in the way you want. This is vital, since your presentation will be building up to this finale, and you need to feel confident that you are not going to fluff it.

This threefold approach is a sound and proven formula for this type of formal presentation:

- tell them what you are going to say
- tell them
- tell them what you have said

Presentation area

You may or may not have direct control over the area where you are going to give your presentation. It might be easier if you are doing it within your own organisation, but even if you are doing it outside, in a hotel for example, when you come to set up or view your presentation area, consider the following:

Seating

Do you want your group to be seated at chairs and tables? Would you prefer them seated around a solid boardroom type table, or would you like the more open horseshoe arrangement? Sometimes a large group is divided into smaller groups, each seated at separate tables around the room. You must decide which is right for your particular presentation.

If you want the group members to make notes, or if your presentation is part of a longer course in which they are involved, you may feel it is advisable for them to have a surface to write on.

If you consider chairs only to be sufficient; will you want this seating to be set out in rows, as in a theatre? This arrangement means that you can accommodate more people than if tables are involved. Rows of chairs can be suitable if your presentation is 'one way', that is, you presenting information to them, without the necessity for them to discuss it among themselves. Bear in mind you cannot run a satisfactory discussion with people sitting in rows (see Chapter 10 – Chairing a Discussion Group).

It might be possible to have chairs set out in a semi-circle, so that members of the group can see each other as well as you, as they would when seated round the horseshoe table. As before, you must decide what is right for your presentation. Do not be afraid to alter a room that is pre-set if you think it is not correctly laid out.

While viewing your presentation area, check that there are no pillars or anything else obstructing the view between the group, you and any visual aid you will want them to see, like an overhead projector screen or a flipboard.

Lighting

Do not underestimate how important the level of lighting is to a presentation. Consider the following points in relation to your presentation area by looking at the lighting – is it:

- too bright?
- too dull?

and is there anything you can do about it, particularly if it is artificial? The intensity of any natural light will probably depend on what the weather is like outside. Make sure that you do not position yourself in front of the window, so that the group members, in facing you, are also facing the daylight. This can be very irritating, and if it is too bright outside, you could appear to them merely as a silhouette. It can also be a strain on their eyes. If, for some reason, the presentation area has to be set out that way round, it would be better to draw the blinds and work in artificial light, if necessary, than to make group members look into a bright light for a period of time – it will not help them to concentrate on what you are saying.

Heating and ventilation

The heat of the room and the condition of the air within it can have a great bearing on how effective your presentation is likely to be from your group's point of view. If the room temperature is extreme, one way or the other, more than likely your listeners are going to be distracted by it. If this is caused by draughts of air, of whatever temperature, from the ventilation ducts, this will be another distraction – particularly if accompanied by noisy fans. This is a delicate subject; for a room which may seem a little cool on arrival will soon warm up when populated by a group of people all generating body heat.

It is an aspect of a presentation which it is all too easy to overlook until it begins to be too late. Make friends with the person who controls the heating and ventilation – or find out how to control it yourself.

Noise

We live in a world of constant noise. Pause now in your reading, and listen to the noises going on around you – both inside and outside the building. In our everyday activities we often have the ability to filter out unwanted noise from what we are doing.

If we are consciously trying to concentrate on a speaker in a formal presentation, we can be all-too-aware of distracting noise. As that speaker, you may be concentrating so much on what you are doing that you are unaware of what is intruding on your group's concentration.

As we said in Chapter 10 – Chairing a Discussion Group, you must be alert at all times to the response you are getting from your group. So, in this more formal situation, you must still glean what feedback you can from your listeners, and a distraction caused by noise could be one such case.

You must be alert to the fact that doing something about that intrusive noise might have an effect on some of the other aspects we have been considering, eg if you close a window to shut out the noise, will the room become too hot? If you open the window because the room *is* too hot, will the noise become unbearable? You might feel like asking 'Can I win?' Very likely not, entirely; but your group will surely appreciate your concern.

Paper and pens

Paper and pens set out neatly on the table at the various places where people will sit make the room look welcoming, and may help convince your group members – especially the early arrivals – that they have come to the right place, and that they are expected. A warning note about pens: if you are providing these, avoid those with spring tops. A group around a table unconsciously clicking their pens as they listen to you can sound like cicadas on a humid night in the tropics – and be very distracting to you as well!

Ashtrays

If smoking is permitted when your presentation is taking place, see that decent ashtrays are provided. Empty them during the coffee or tea breaks or at lunchtime – or see that it is done. Overflowing ashtrays do nothing for the appearance of your presentation area.

As you can see, there is quite a lot to consider when setting up the area where you are going to make your presentation. What you are really doing is setting the scene, and if the surroundings are inviting, this will help your audience get into the right frame of mind to accept you and what you have to present to them. It will also help you show your self presentation skills off to advantage. So, make sure that everything to be used or demonstrated can be seen by each member of the group. Sit in the farthest and nearest chairs yourself to check that the line of sight is not blocked.

Check your personal appearance; anything untidy or out of keeping could be distracting, and the group might pay more attention to that than what you are saying.

Presentation

If you feel nervous at the thought of speaking formally in front of a group of people, do not worry; many people do, including experienced speakers. Your adequate preparation will help to give you that feeling of confidence: you know what you are going to talk about, and that you have a sensible set of notes to keep you on course.

There are several ways to gain the attention of your group when you are ready to begin your presentation:

- ask a question
- make a profound or 'dramatic' statement
- write an interesting heading on the flipboard
- display an eye-catching visual on the OHP screen
- produce an intriguing visual aid

Once your group appreciates that you have started, give a general indication of the purpose of your presentation. Do not plunge straight into detail, but give your listeners a broad outline and general background of what will be covered, to give them a chance to appreciate what is wanted of them.

Your attitude at this early stage is important. Although you have thoroughly researched your subject, avoid giving the impression that you know it all. On the other hand, as you begin your presentation, *never apologise* to the group members for their having to put up with you, even if you say it in fun. Do not say it at all. Whatever you are feeling inside, in the eyes of the group you are the expert. If you start apologising, they will begin to feel that they are getting second best, and wonder why they do not justify having the real expert to give the presentation. So, do not begin with what is often just a nervous remark, because it could alienate your audience, and then you have the extra struggle of winning over their confidence as well as making your presentation effective.

We recommend three components for an effective presentation:

- poise
- pace
- pitch

Poise

Try to stand comfortably and naturally, with your hands by your sides (see Chapter 1 – Body Language). This is often difficult to do when you become conscious of your arms and hands.

Have your notes readily to hand. If necessary, hold them in your hands rather than have them resting on the table, which would mean you looking down towards the table rather than out at your audience. A suitable compromise, if you did not want to hold your notes, would be to put them on a raised surface such as a lectern placed on the table top. If, as a temporary measure, you decide an upside down cardboard box would do the job, cover it with a sheet of plain (flipboard) paper to make it look a little presentable.

Speak directly to your listeners, looking at all of them (embrace the group) rather than at a spot on the ceiling, or into one corner of the room above their heads. Beware of the temptation to address all your remarks to a friendly face in the group, to the exclusion of the others, who might begin to wonder why they came.

Having got your hands and arms under control, try not to fidget on your feet, and avoid excessive movement. If you are a man, avoid jangling coins in your trouser pockets. If you are a women, avoid wearing jangling jewellery on your wrists – both can be unbearably distracting for listeners.

Avoid ungainly postures (see Chapter 1 – Body Language) and irritating mannerisms (see Chapter 12 – Media Interviews), although the controlled use of gesture can be effective. Remember, if you are standing behind a table, that the group can probably see your legs and feet, particularly if the table is on a raised platform or stage. Beware of any unintentional ballet-like movements, which could cause distracting amusement to your group.

Pace

Start slowly. Having your introduction written out in full will help to prevent you from galloping away from the starting point, which can sometimes be a symptom of apprehension or nerves. You should, of course, vary the pace at which you make your presentation. This will often be determined by what you have to say.

If you have something exciting to put across, you will naturally tend to speak faster than if you are making a straightforward and factual statement. Do not go to the other extreme, of course, and make it sound dull and boring.

Since you will know in advance what you are going to say in your presentation, you will be able to decide which points need to be emphasised. Think of emphasis as verbal punctuation; so it needs to be correct. Incorrect emphasis, or the misplacing of a word, can entirely alter the sense of a statement. For example:

'I'm going to go through *this* report' (not the other one), means something quite different from 'I'm going to go through this *report*' – as opposed to this letter, this questionnaire, etc.

'Give the draft to one agency only' means something different from 'Only give the draft to one agency' or 'Give the only draft to one agency'.

Avoid a steady, plodding, dismal tone throughout your presentation, although the facts which need to be emphasised should be spoken slowly to ensure that the point is made.

Using a variety of inflection will help to make your voice sound interesting. Certain things naturally lend themselves to a pattern of inflection. For example, questions always end on a rising inflection. Try asking a few and hear what we mean.

Do not be afraid to pause to look at your notes: no-one is going to think any the worse of you for that. After all, you are not acting a role, where all the words need to be learned in advance. A well-chosen pause has many advantages; apart from giving your audience a rest from listening to you. A pause enables you to begin again at a different tempo, which gives variety to your presentation as a whole.

There is a skill in knowing how long to hold a pause to gain maximum effect. This can only be learned through practical experience, but it is worth experimenting, because it is very satisfying when it works.

For example, if you can bring yourself to hold a pause after you have made an important point or statement, you will find it gives your audience time to appreciate the significance of what you have just said. Mark your notes with a pause sign ∩, to remind you where it should come.

Pitch

Pitching your voice does not mean shouting: this can be ineffective and counter-productive. Your aim during your presentation should be to control the pitch or level of your voice so that everybody can hear what you are saying. The degree of pitch required depends quite a lot on your surroundings. For example, curtains and carpet tend to deaden the sound by absorption, and cut out any echo. You will find that in these surroundings you can speak relatively quietly and still be heard.

A lack of furnishings encourages resonance. Think of how voices echo around an empty room, and the difference when the furniture is in and the curtains are hung up. If you find yourself in a place which echoes (a staff canteen with lino tiles, perhaps), you must allow for this. Speaking more slowly and clearly and not too loudly might help. Remember, though, it might be easier than you thought once your group members are there, because they will absorb the sound to some extent. So, it might not be as bad as you feared when you tested the acoustic in the 'unpopulated' room. The first step towards curing an acoustic problem is being aware of it.

What will help you to make sure you are heard and understood is to avoid being lazy in the way you speak during your presentation. For example:

- avoid mumbling
- avoid dropping your voice at the end of a sentence
- avoid slurring words together
- avoid speaking too softly or too loudly.

Attention to these points will help to prevent your listeners from losing interest.

If you can achieve a warm, friendly voice, this will hold the attention of your listeners and help you get over the effect you want. One way of helping yourself use your voice to the best advantage is to hear yourself as others hear you, by listening to yourself on a cassette recorder (see also Chapter 3 – Oral Assessment and Chapter 12 – Media Interviews). After the initial shock, this exercise will help you to highlight areas of possible improvement. We all like to think that we have pleasant speaking voices, so it can come as rather a surprise if we hear ourselves sounding brusque or unfriendly.

Insincerity is something which shows through: you must convey a sincere interest and conviction in what you are saying, otherwise your presentation will never achieve the impact you want.

Feedback

We pointed out at the beginning of this chapter that a disadvantage of this type of formal presentation techniques is that your audience do not have to give any evidence of accepting what you say. It is therefore essential that you glean what feedback you can from your audience as your presentation progresses. This is one of the reasons why this type of presentation is so tiring, because you cannot afford to switch off for a moment. You need to keep your eye out for responses such as:

- signs of restlessness
- fidgeting with pens, papers
- private conversations breaking out
- negative body language (see Chapter 1 – Body Language)

Remedies

If you spot some of these signs of flagging, what can you do to regain the interest of your group? You could:

- produce a visual aid (something to attract their attention)

- write up something relevant on the flipboard (something to focus on)
- display a sample object (to help clarify something you are saying)
- ask the group a general question (they may not have understood something)
- pause (effective for stopping private conversations; takes courage at first)
- continue with renewed vigour and enthusiasm (take a deep breath and grit your teeth)

Effective ending

Give thought to the way you are going to end your presentation, so that you can work up to an effective conclusion. There is nothing much more disappointing than a presentation which just fizzles out like a damp squib. There is a danger, though, that once your listeners realise that you are into your big finish, they will begin to pack up their papers and look at their watches to see whether they will be in time to catch the next train, or beat the rush hour traffic.

It is even more vital to finish effectively if the main purpose of your presentation is to inspire action on the part of your listeners once you have finished eg a sales drive or a special task to be done.

Make a final summary of what you have said, and round off with a firm conclusive sentence. As with your introduction, having your conclusion written out in full will help you to achieve the effect you want.

If you are given a set time for your presentation, make sure you keep to it. Put your watch or a small clock on the table where you can see it.

 After sales service

Dependent on the circumstances, it might be desirable to hand out a printed summary to your listeners as a memory jogger. This could be particularly useful if they are to put into action themselves what you have covered in your presentation. Do not hand papers out in the middle of a presentation unless you want the group to refer to them at that time.

128

Discussion

It might be relevant to allow time after your formal presentation for a period of questions and discussion. If you intend to do this, it is worth saying so at the beginning of your presentation, so that members of the group will know that they will have the opportunity of raising or clarifying any points after you have finished.

Visual aids

Visual aids are really additional methods of communication, and can be very useful in making a presentation that much more effective. They can take many forms and have a variety of uses, so it is necessary to consider which is the correct and most appropriate visual aid to use in any given situation.

It is important to remember that they are *aids* to an effective presentation and you should not allow them to take over, to the detriment of the presentation as a whole, so that the group remembers the *aid* and not the message it was being used to support.

You could use a visual aid to:
- attract attention and gain the interest of the group
- hold the attention of the group while you describe something complicated
- give information in a straightforward way
- illustrate relationships otherwise difficult to explain
- involve the group to help their understanding
- underline, emphasise or enforce a specific point you want to make
- sum up and recap on what you have covered in your presentation.

If you intend to use visual aids, make sure that they are properly prepared. Set them out in the right order before you begin your presentation, so that you can use them quickly and effectively when the time comes. Write in your notes where you are to produce a visual aid and, equally important, when you want to get rid of it.

Take care of your visual aids if you are going to repeat your presentation, and you will know that they are in good condition and ready for use.

Post mortem

Try to spend a moment or two after your presentation is over
deciding why it went the way it did – for good or ill. Use this
knowledge to help you with your next presentation.

Points to remember from this chapter

- Study and digest the subject of your presentation
- Consider the composition of your audience and why they need
  to know what you are going to say
- Be clear about the sequence of your main points
- Make notes and do not hesitate to refer to them
- Prepare visual aids thoroughly
- Prepare the presentation area suitably
- Pay attention to your personal appearance
- Start slowly and vary the pace during your presentation
- Be sincere and show conviction in your subject
- Conclude in an effective way
- Keep to the allotted time, if applicable

12 Media Interviews

In front of the camera or microphone

If you are called on for the first time to represent your organisation in a media interview, perhaps as part of a local or national news bulletin or current affairs programme, how do you feel? Probably pleased and apprehensive at the same time. This chapter is to help you prepare yourself as well as possible to appear in front of the cameras or microphone.

There are two broad categories of interview under this heading;

- the more formal type of interview arranged in advance, held in a studio, or, perhaps, in the interviewee's office.
- the kerbside interview, where an interviewee is tackled on the pavement before or after a meeting, or following an incident in which the organisation or other body has been involved, or about which the interviewee has specific or specialist knowledge. The interviewee is expected to respond off the cuff to the interviewer, armed at least with a microphone, but often supported by a mobile ENG (Electronic News Gathering) camera balanced on the cameraman's shoulder.

This chapter covers the implications of each of these categories for the interviewee, and the organisation or body being represented.

Pre-arranged interviews

Your local radio or television station might approach you for an interview about some topic of interest relating to your organisation or sphere of work. It could be something to do with a special event planned by your business, a publicity visit by a showbiz celebrity, or a possible change in trading policy with local implications. It could be related to the activities of the Students' Union or similar body involved in a matter of topical or local interest.

How would you react to this? Would it frighten you stiff? Would you feel confident that you would do it without any trouble? Perhaps a feeling somewhere between those two. Whatever your reaction, it needs thinking about because, apart from any feelings you may have about it personally, good or bad, remember it is an opportunity to gain some free publicity for your organisation or cause.

The cost of advertising for a period of time similar to your interview, say 3–4 minutes with any luck, could run into four figures. So it is an opportunity well worth grasping with both hands in order to create good publicity and goodwill among the listeners or viewers.

Establish the situation

As with any form of presentation, careful preparation before the event pays off at the time. Preparation begins by establishing which programme will be carrying your interview. Because it is likely to be your local radio or TV station, you may well be familiar with the sort of programme it is. If not, try to make a point of listening to, or watching, a few editions to get the feel of its character and style, and in particular how the interviewers work. Find out what type of audience it is likely to attract, and what time of day the interview will be broadcast or screened; the two are bound to be linked.

A vital point to find out very early on is how long the interview will be *when it is actually broadcast or screened:* you cannot really do any sensible preparation until this is quite clearly established. We shall return to this point again shortly.

Try to clarify what questions you are going to be asked. If for any reason you cannot be told the exact questions, insist at least on an indication of the topics to be discussed.

Find out what form the interview will take. There are several alternatives:

- It might be recorded or broadcast live
  - if recorded; will it be recorded at the studio, in your office, on location somewhere within your organisation, like a workshop or outside in the car park? It could be recorded over the telephone, if it is to be a sound only interview
  - if live; will it be from the studio, with you and the interviewer there together, or via a telephone link with the interviewer in one studio and you elsewhere, perhaps in another studio, or in your own office?

Having established at least some of those facts, you are now in a position to do some material preparation.

Know your subject

The essential element to a successful media interview is to know what you are talking about, and to be seen to know what you are talking about. We cannot emphasise too strongly that it is absolute suicide to try to talk about something in a media interview with which you are not fully familiar or do not believe in. It is better to delegate the interview to somebody who has specialised knowledge of the subject, rather than try to flannel through on your own. Your inadequacy or insincerity will shine out like a beacon, and it will not do you or the organisation or movement you represent any good at all, so, know your subject – thoroughly.

Even if you do know your subject inside out – and you will not be doing this interview otherwise will you! – it is very useful to make brief notes, preferably just headings, on points you want to make: key words. Remember, you will be in a strange environment, and you could be put off your stroke by the unexpected. Read the glossary of terms at the end of this chapter; it will help to familiarise you with some of what is going on around you.

If you have established exactly how long the broadcast interview is likely to last, you can decide how much you can get across in the time – probably only two or three really important points. Jotting down the odd key word on a card, which you can have readily in front of you, keeps you to those essential points; and *essential points* is a phrase of much importance. Decide which points it is absolutely essential that you make. List them in order, and add one or two *desirable* points in case you find you have a little time in hand – which is unlikely.

Thinking things through at this stage will save you trouble, and the pain of kicking yourself afterwards for not having made the one point you felt was essential to the whole subject.

Prepare yourself

Having prepared your material, the time has now come to think about preparing the person. A media interview could be likened to an appraisal interview, with *you* in the appraisee's chair. Imagine that situation, but replace the word interview with 'discussion', with the other person asking the leading questions. Imagine you are having a discussion in your office with one of your colleagues.

Well, why not *have* a discussion in your office with one of your colleagues and, with his or her consent, have a cassette recorder on the desk? The result will provide you with an excellent basis for self questioning:
- does my recorded voice sound acceptable?
- do I convey a favourable personality?
- do I sound (and if you have access to a video camera and recorder, look) interested in what I am saying?
- is what I am saying likely to be interesting to the listener or viewer?
- is what I am saying likely to be easily understood, both in terms of content and clarity of speech?

The advantage of using the (audio/video) recorder approach in your preparation is that you can hear and/or see yourself as you sound or appear to others. Rather a shock the first time around, but in the privacy of your own home, you can try out for yourself various ideas you may have for improving on what you see or hear. You can also rehearse the sort of general answers you want to give, using your key word card as an aide memoire. Do not, however, learn an answer parrot-fashion, because you may be asked the question in a slightly different way, which might mean altering the tense – not the sense – of your reply. But, if you know your subject, you will be able to respond in the way most appropriate to the phrasing of the question.

You are probably no stranger to communication; perhaps your job demands it of you all the time. The microphone and/or the camera, as the all-hearing ear and all-seeing eye respectively, unlike the selective ear and eye of the listener and viewer, is an unsympathetic, but realistic interpreter of fact. The microphone particularly, if unaccompanied by a visual image, will not filter out the errors, the unpleasant tone of voice, as the human ear does. Whatever you say into a microphone comes out again in exactly the same way in which you said it – faults and all.

Do remember that, in the situation we are thinking about, especially the audio only interview, it is your voice, and your voice *only*, which is your ambassador. *You* are not there, in the sense that you cannot be seen by your listeners; they can only judge on what they hear, and build up their own mental picture. So, how can your ambassador create for you the image that you want to impress on the minds of the listeners, bearing in mind the value of the free advertising opportunity for your organisation this interview is giving?

With a television interview, the viewers will be able to see you as well as hear you. Some of the principles for being a successful job applicant, which we covered in Chapter 4 – At a Job Interview, could apply equally well here, particularly those about appearance and bearing: it is just that the pressure might be greater!

Earlier we suggested that you think of this interview as a discussion with a colleague in the office. Think of it rather as a discussion under a microscope. Do the recording exercise as suggested, and when you play it back, as well as doing the self-questioning exercise, see how you match up to the following checklist:

- do you drop your voice at the end of sentences, so that the final, and perhaps vital, word is missed by the listener?
- do you omit the 't' for example from the end of words? The casual way we often carry on normal face-to-face conversations does not make for effective interview listening. Simple things like paying attention to the 't's and 'd's on the ends of words will make a world of difference to the way the listener comprehends what you are saying. Really listen to top broadcasters; they make it sound easy and casual, but you can hear the techniques if you consciously listen.

Another distraction which is likely to create a barrier between you and your listeners' comprehension, is verbal mannerisms. Things like, 'you know', 'I mean', 'so', 'obviously', 'that's right', 'no way', 'there you go' and the perennial, 'at this moment in time'. You can probably think of some current ones: maybe you use some of them yourself; but 'hopefully' not. The repeated use of these words and phrases, while perhaps not so noticeable in normal face-to-face communication, becomes very intrusive when heard on radio, as does a string of 'erms' and 'ahs'; all detracting from the essential message you want to get across.

If you have done some practice videos, see what your mannerisms are, both physical and verbal. Decide what you can do to overcome them, but try not to become paranoid about them, just keep them in check, before they become a distraction to the listeners or viewers.

People often listen to the radio while doing something else; for example, when driving a car where you cannot – or should not – give your *full* attention to the radio. So, the clearer your message comes across, the more likely you are to achieve your target: the effective communication of your remarks or message.

One way of making sure that you come over distinctly is not to speak too quickly. Sounds obvious: it is; but not so easy to put into practice. Being nervous, or at least apprehensive – and it never does any good going into this sort of thing in an over-confident frame of mind – tends to make you talk faster than in normal circumstances: incidentally, so does arriving at the studio at the last minute in an agitated state.

Your key word card will now come into its own. Let it remind you of the subject you are going to talk about, and then calmly put over the facts you want, steadily and firmly.

One final word on preparation – write it on your key word card: DRINK. Keep off intoxicating drink before your interview, whether this is taking place at a studio or in your own office. By all means have one afterwards to celebrate, but go into the interview itself with a clear head, a clear idea of what you want to say, and clear articulation with which to say it – effectively. Believe what you say and be yourself. Your sincerity and personality will help to ensure clear, effective communication between you and your listeners or viewers, through the expertise of your interviewer.

 ## Kerbside interviews

If you want to talk to reporters 'off the cuff', fair enough. Stop and give them a proper interview. Make sure you have the authority to speak on behalf of your organisation or body to which you belong. If you do not want to talk to reporters, say nothing and keep walking. It is difficult to do sometimes, but possible, and if you say nothing, you will not say anything out of place.

Know your subject

As with a pre-arranged interview, do not try to talk about something you do not know about or do not believe in; incompetence or insincerity will show. A kerbside interview is a good publicity opportunity, but it is better not to say anything than make a hash of it.

Getting your points across

Kerbside interviews are usually a very brief part of a news or current affairs programme, and much of what you say is likely to be edited out. Decide quickly on not more than two important points you want to make; if you try to make too many points, you are likely to confuse the listeners or viewers, and the ones actually selected for transmission might not be the most important from your point of view.

Respond, as far as you can, to the questions actually asked by the interviewer, but be careful not to say anything which could be misinterpreted or is too controversial. What you say is being recorded, and could be used again. This is why professional communicators, like politicians, often seem irritatingly bland in their replies; they are skilled in not saying things which will land them in hot water later on.

Nevertheless, if you have something important to say, say it firmly and with conviction, and you will do the organisation or the people you are representing a power of good. Keep the listeners and viewers on your side:

- do not be aggressive
- do not be rude
- do not swear (it is likely to be edited out anyway)
- do not flannel
- keep calm: if you get too excited you will not be understood

You cannot do a lot of preparation for this type of interview. You might gain a little time if you are invited outside to do a 'kerbside', as distinct from being stopped in the street or as you leave the building. The best you can do in any case is to know your subject, know your own mind and be yourself.

Glossary of terms

AUTOCUE:	screen from which professionals 'read' what they have to say
CLIP MIKE:	small mike clipped onto lapel; also called LAPEL MIKE
CUE:	signal to start transmission or recording
DIRECTOR:	person actually in control of the technical output
EDITOR:	person who decides on the content and running order
E N G:	electronic news gathering (video camera)
FEEDBACK:	screeches or squeaks in the sound transmission
FLOOR MANAGER:	person in control on the studio floor
FLUFF:	stumbling over words
HANDHELD:	microphone held in the interviewer's hand
IDENT:	identification of a particular recording
INTRO:	introductory sequence, music etc
LAPEL MIKE:	*see* CLIP MIKE
LIVE:	actually broadcast at the time of speaking
ON AIR:	broadcast in progress
ON LINE:	interviewer in the studio; interviewee in a different place
OUTRO:	finishing sequence, music etc
POPPING:	talking too closely into the microphone
PRODUCER:	person controlling the programme
TALK BACK:	talking to the studio from the control room
TO CAMERA:	talking directly to the camera
VOICE CHECK:	used to establish the level of the voice when speaking into the microphone
VOX POP:	interviews with the 'man in the street'
WIND UP:	instruction to the interviewer from the director or editor to close the interview at the next convenient point

Points to remember from this chapter

General preparation
- Radio or television?
- Which programme?
- What time is the broadcast or screening?
- What type of audience?
- How long will the interview be when broadcast or screened?
- What questions will be asked? or
- Indication of topics to be covered
- Will the interview go out live or will it be pre-recorded?

Material preparation
- Know your subject – or delegate the interview
- Key word card – for essential points (plus desirables, just in case)

Personal preparation
- Record practice discussion
- Act on response to self-questioning
- Control verbal and/or physical mannerisms
- Do not drink beforehand

Objective
- Be yourself, be sincere
- Believe in what you say

Index